Simple Methods for

Detecting Buying and

Selling Points

In Securities

James Liveright

First Published 1926
by Ticker Publishing Company
New York

Fraser Publishing Company Edition
©Fraser Publishing Company 1968
Wells, Vermont

Second Printing, 1984

ISBN: 0-87034-028-X
Library of Congress Catalog Card Number: 68-21699
Printed in the U.S.A.

CONTENTS

Introduction

Fundamental Principles That the Reader and
Student Should Keep in Mind............ 5

Chapters

   I How to Detect Accumulation........ 17

  II How to Detect the End of Accumu-
      lation 27

 III When to Buy and When to Sell..... 37

 IV How to Analyze Market Swings...... 55

  V How to Gauge the Technical Position . 67

 VI How to Detect Turning Points...... 87

VII How to Detect Liquidation.......... 99

VIII How to Detect Short Selling........ 109

 IX How to Detect Pool Operations...... 121

FOREWORD

This is a reprint of the 3rd edition of a Wall Street classic. Often we forget that the fundamentals of investment and speculation are simple. Though markets evolve, common stock is still a commodity with ownership crystallized into a single certificate quoted at a definite price. As time passes, the demand for the supply of stocks can be interpreted if not regulated. The examples on the following pages are from a market period that differs from today though the spirit of speculation then and now appears similar.

James L. Fraser
Wells, Vermont

INTRODUCTION

Fundamental Principles That the Reader and Student Should Keep in Mind

PROFESSOR NEWTON evolved the theory of action and reaction as applied to the science of mechanics, and from this has been built up many applications and variations of the theory. It is said to apply with similar effect on business, economics, and human intercourse.

Whether or not it is a perfect guide to the science of making money *via* the stock market is debatable, and not altogether relevant. The supporters of the theory are limited to the assumption that history not only repeats itself, but that it is bound to do so in the future, and will continue going back in its tracks to the end of time. Charts showing security averages, business cycles, money yields (based on prime bonds), bank clearings and the like are kept and quoted with enough authority to lend considerable color to the "action and reaction" theory and the reader should under-

5

stand its broad purport, not merely for its academic interest, but because so many are actuated by its curves, its broad and short swings, and its reasonable similarity to its predecessors, that if it does nothing else but help us *anticipate* how very many people of substantial means will be actuated—a month, two months, or six months hence—we can act bright and early, and secure an early advantage by anticipating the *demand* for securities, and being on the job with a good *supply* when there are temporarily more sellers than buyers.

We stress the advantage of anticipating coming movements. The homely old saying "It's the early bird that catches the worm," trite and bromidic as it sounded in our post-graduation days, has a wealth of meaning in the stock market, as we will show later.

What are securities and what do they stand for?

Let it be understood that we are referring throughout this little work to the common stocks of American corporations, and not to bonds, preferred stocks, specialty issues, or the more closely held bank, insurance, trust, textile mills, and similar securities. The latter are not widely held; they are not capable of general manipulation, and nothing but the known economic factors can affect them.

They offer little or nothing to the average speculator (and by this term we include the investor who
is not averse to taking a speculative position occasionally); and by the exclusion of "the public"
are not susceptible of big swings, profit making
advances or declines, activity, volume, and relative
frequency so necessary to worth-while trading.

Common Stocks as the Owner's Share

Common stocks are certificates that crystallize
equities in every class and type of industry known
to man. They represent the owner's share in so
many miles of railroad, so many tons of copper,
so many barrels of oil; or as many pairs of shoes,
bales of wool, tons of hides, or kegs of tobacco,
together with his share of the steel mills, turbines,
buildings, plant, cash, receivables. They represent
the assumed value as things are valued *to-day*, plus
something added for earning power for an indef-
inite period ahead. As valuations fluctuate almost
daily, as they differ according to the opinions of
their appraisers (the buyers and sellers), and as
different local, countrywide, and international conditions change hourly with the news reported in the
newspapers, so different interpretations by thousands of men and women widely separated through-

out the world stamp the concensus of the *average general opinion* in one crystallized written verdict.

U. S. Steel is quoted on the tape $88 a share as this is written, and regardless of statistics, your opinion, my opinion, or the belief of the man in the street, buyers and sellers are united in believing at this moment that the owner of one share of U. S. Steel has $88 worth of value in hand for $88 paid. Neither book values far higher than this, nor safe dividends, nor the belief that dividends may be higher later enter into this figure at this moment. U. S. Steel common has become *a commodity;* its ownership is a combined investment crystallized into a single certificate quoted at a definite figure, in so many miles of railroad, so many tons of rails, pig iron, mined and unmined ore, coal, ships, machinery, cash, securities, and the thousand and one things that make the composite "Steel Corporation."

Why does U. S. Steel sell at $88? Why not at $100 or $50? Why does it not sell near its book value, appraised at over $250 a share? Why does it fluctuate in market value $7 to $10 a share in a comparatively few weeks, which cannot be due to changing values of such proportions in so little time?

Subject to Face of Supply and Demand

This brings us to a contemplation of the basic structure of this as well as every other market, the understanding of which would lead to more profits and less losses. Considering securities as commodities (or their equivalent), as tangible certificates of money value they are subject to the basic law of supply and demand. The buying and selling of securities is purely a business proposition, and as such is amenable to no other rule but that of being wanted at a price, and being offered for sale at a price. A stock is worth no more than buyers are willing to pay for it at this moment; it will not bring more than it is offered for in the open markets—the stock exchanges throughout the country. It matters not *why* they wish to buy, whether they be investors (individuals, banks, institutions, capitalists, or insiders), speculators, or professional traders "short" and desirous of covering. The reasons are seldom apparent; *the price is*. We may deduce the reasons, or approximate them by studying the tape and the market. Conversely, it matters not why selling pressure exists. It matters very much that we know that the number and importance (in dollars) of sellers exceeds buyers, because when the selling ceases buyers will again predominate, and prices will go up. *This is certain!*

The state of flux or balance—more buyers than sellers; more sellers than buyers—leads to a certain situation from which a movement upward or downward can be expected. It leads to a *technical position* where a change of trend is imminent. We can often judge whether such a change will be of large proportion; at times it is more difficult, and at times frankly impossible when our mental attitude is best left open and neutral.

Importance of Technical Position

The ability to judge the technical position, the balance of fact and probability as between the mass of buyers and sellers, and the ability to act promptly, decisively, and confidently is the difference between the successful investor and speculator who stays in Wall Street a whole lifetime, and the novice who may make a few dollars by being a bull in a bull market, and then getting more bullish on top of a market that looks strong to the public, and sitting tight on a really weak technical position where the first harsh whisper from influential quarters serves to topple the whole structure.

The technical position works by contrasts. As the

witty Mr. Dooley says: *"Panics are th' result of too many people having money. Th' top iv good times is hard times an' th' bottom iv hard times is good times."* Mr. Dooley means to tell you that too much money leads to inflation; inflation causes surface prosperity but a weak technical position for business. Deflation is the natural remedy and consequence, as sure as reaction follows action in mechanics. *"Th' bottom iv hard times"* is the time when only rich men, capitalists, institutions, and insiders (let's be quite frank in calling the shovels just "spades") generally hold the stocks, or are busy accumulating them, and this creates an invulnerable technical position. The bottom of a bear market finds securities on the peak of a strong technical position, and this position becomes gradually weakened as stocks go up. Conversely, a terrific rise creates a weak technical position *invariably* (there are no exceptions to this rule) and its weakness bears a direct relationship to the time consumed between bottom and top, the class of stocks that rose, the extent of manipulation, the class of buyers, and the class of insiders tempted to sell—and who likely have sold out on the rise.

Mr. Dooley makes a further sage remark that we will quote as indicating a weakened technical position in *production.* *"When I see wan man with a shovel on his shoulder dodgin' eight thousand autymobills I begin to think 'tis time to put me money in me boot."*

The sagacious Mr. Dooley is using horse sense to convey that if a single man is producing so that eight thousand may ride, consume gas, and burn up the roads, the technical position of business and production has reached a dangerous point; in fact so dangerous that he wouldn't even trust the banks who have financed the auto, oil and gas companies. It is *so* in the stock market. When one sees the speculators in control, which is apparent to the student in the many ways we will endeavor to point out later; when one sees the big interests, the solid investors, the producers getting out and cashing in, we ought to know that the reaction is going to follow unproductive or over-stimulated action. At such times we must avoid buying that which the other man is pressing for sale, even at apparent bargain-counter levels, on the assumption that every decline will run its proper course regardless of temporary stimulation, artificial price changes, or theories as to the future based on past performances which might have no application to the present set of conditions.

Finally, by way of asking the reader's indulgence
to accept this contribution to financial research in
the sincere hope that it will contribute to his en-
lightenment and understanding of the things that
are "Wall Street," and to his ultimate comfort (and
perhaps greater material profit), the thought is
dominant in my mind that a man or woman gets
out of most things—in life as well as the stock
market—an equivalent measure of the things put in.
We have seen the competent statistician and student
of security values rely almost solely on his keen
analyses of values taking an occasional investment
position in the stocks he had judged to be sound,
and year after year with only small losses, retire
with a handsome competence. But it is the work
of a lifetime to become such a good and accurate
judge. We have also seen the investor and speculator with a lesser knowledge of statistics, but with
a general perception of sound business doctrines,
and an ability to sift the wheat from the chaff in
the way of facts and probabilities, do as well both
as an investor and trader. We have also seen the
technician who judges solely by the technical position, who has made a long study of the problem
and has placed an adequate capital behind his trading ventures, retire from the field with no mean

accumulation of profits. In every case, preliminary and conscientious study was a big ingredient in the factors that made for success.

It is impossible to represent that any one book or work can be more than a stepping-stone to higher studies. Each can implant a little more knowledge that will encourage further research and observation. In time, the precepts from all of them, if clearly and concisely set forth, will be translated into action at a critical time that may spell success or defeat, according to the amount of effort put in. The author has read and studied practically every book and publication ever put out by *The Magazine of Wall Street*, and freely acknowledges the valuable hints and suggestions, not directly quoted here, but subconsciously remembered and retained. After all, few things are really original. There are but seven notes in the octave and twenty-six letters in the alphabet; just a handful of basic colors in the spectrum. Yet what a wealth of music, literature, and art is built on such a primitive beginning. The fundamentals of security investment and speculation are as simple. To violate them is to invite defeat before the race is even begun. To know thoroughly those fundamentals that have served faithfully during a hundred years or more in our markets (methods do not change radically) and to regulate our actions according to this knowledge, is to take the first step towards becoming, not perhaps another Gould, Keene or Livermore, but certainly an investor or speculator who is endeavoring to keep in harmony with the trend of conditions, and to abide by the technical position as he conceives it.

CHAPTER I

How to Detect Accumulation

The Meaning of Accumulation and Conditions Under Which These Operations Can Be Detected

BEFORE we can profit by any knowledge as to market technique it is as well to learn (to use a colloquialism) "what it is all about."

To accumulate is to acquire *gradually*. Cases arise where an inside interest—commonly called insiders—may find it convenient to accumulate, to acquire, in a hurry. But these interests do not often work hurriedly. We'll cite instances and also the special technique and operations where *the* pool bought hurriedly, tried to distribute rapidly, and failed hopelessly, all within a period of a few months.

Accumulating, then, as we know it and understand it, is the process of getting a long position; of going long; or as the reader would erroneously say, "of buying"—a line of stock. Distinguish,

17

however, at the very outset between plain buying and accumulating. They are as far apart as the heavens.

Let me quote from a conversation between two veterans of the Street, a conversation that took place in the late winter of 1921. You will remember that U. S. Steel was again in the lower 80s, recovering from a long decline, a drop of the largest proportion since its war and post-war boom that put it up from the 50s to above 135, down to the lower 90s, and twice well above par. This time it had dropped from 116 to below 80 in the general smash of late lamented memory between 1920 and 1922.

"What's your idea about Steel?" the one veteran asked the other. "They're buying on balance, and not too anxious to bid it up!" The veterans agreed. "What then?" the questioner asked. "Oh well, I expect distribution above par unless the public runs away with it."

A more detailed explanation of what "they" were doing, according to the veteran (whose judgment proved uncannily correct) would be interesting. We will not digress at this stage by discussing the identity of "they"; indeed it does not matter so long as their operations indicate that they are affiliated with big interests, and financially responsible.

Pools do not usually operate on a shoestring, in U. S. Steel nor in anything else. We are not discussing that kind of pool.

Pool Activities

The pool or the buying interest or interests (there may be several at one time) aims, if it is a bull pool, to accumulate its intended line of stock as cheaply as possible, and to sell out, when the time comes, for as much money as it can get. There is no sentiment about a pool; it is a business proposition; a transaction in merchandising. It aims to lay in a stock of this or that security, to sell the whole or part at a good profit, not necessarily at one time, but all the time, and to be out of its line at the right time, and very often to be short of its stock if necessary for the purpose of giving it support on the decline which is sure to come sooner or later.

The crude, stupid little expression "What goes up must come down; what goes down will go up" is fairly true of the majority of the big active listed stocks (Curb stocks like the Standard Oils are really "listed" on *that* exchange).

Let us then appreciate the function and intention of a pool. Its object is neither charity nor sympathy.

It aims to make money for itself (its members), and its followers. Big pools have a following and a tremendous value if they are identified with success. A one-man pool can also be a big success, and his services sought at his own price. James R. Keene was the one-man pool hired by the Steel Corporations' bankers to make a market for the newly formed combine and to induce exchange of subsidiary stocks for the new parent corporation in 1901. His personal knowledge and following was worth many millions to the big corporation and a fortune to the operator himself. Sometimes they act alone, for their personal profit, in one or more stocks, and even in the entire market. This is illustrated in Edwin LeFevre's book, "Reminiscences of a Stock Operator," a story of Larry Livingston which ran in the Saturday Evening Post, 1922-3. Mr. Livingston is a well-known Wall Street operator whom the writer doesn't think it necessary to advertise further. Suffice it to say he is the modern prototype of Keene and so far almost as spectacular, if not as successful.

The student need waste no time questioning the motive of a pool, nor be concerned with the question whether it is official (allied with inside interests), nor whether it is an inside, outside or bob-tailed (a trailer) pool. There are times when well-placed publicity will indicate its character. On the other hand, one has to judge by the character of its operations whether it is strong, weak, well-informed, or merely "an interest" with money to support its bullishness or bearishness. When in doubt, one has the choice of not following its operations, or if participating, protecting each and every commitment with a stop loss order—a protection that the wise trader should *never be without*.

How the Insiders Commence Operations

Before we can begin to study the art of detecting accumulation it is as well to know how the big interests, the banking interests, the pools, and the so-called insiders go about it, and to do likewise if at all possible.

That which applies to a single stock also applies in general to the entire market, since accumulation on a general scale is no different in effect or method to accumulation of a single stock.

For the sake of simplicity let us follow an imaginary, but we believe typical operation covering the accumulation of "a line" of Reading Company. We will assume that prices of stocks are around the bottom at the end of a bear market that has about run its course, and the interests usually identified with the market in Reading are about ready to take a position (to go long) and give the stock one of its characteristic upswings. At a price between 60 and 65 they believe it will go much higher; that developments in earnings, the rail situation, the coal situation, or a segregation of its coal holdings (a time-worn factor in this case) will give the stock a lot of interest *at higher prices*—sufficient to show a good profit on a market operation after paying all expenses.

The factor of expense in running a pool and conducting a big market operation must not be lost sight of, and market interests are compelled to *accumulate* guardedly, cautiously, and profitably to preserve its very existence. There is no certainty, no guaranty, no sympathy in pool operations. It is a big bet by the bulls concerned with the rest of the world that they will buy cheaply and sell dearly; that they will either clean their shelves of accumulated stocks at a profit and perhaps go short at or around the top, or by the marking down process (applying profits to cost price), acquire a line of investment holdings at an average satisfactory price to the accumulating interest or interests.

Not always do pools aim to make profits in mere

points. They may desire to accumulate in the strict-est sense for the purpose of adding to their own or inside lines. The New York Central may wish to in-crease its line of Reading with some of its surplus funds, and to buy as cheaply as possible. Its presi-dent would not go into the market and write out an order "Buy 100,000 Reading at the market, and send it round by bearer." It isn't done that way. He would likely, after proper authority secured, signed, sealed and delivered, talk it over with the railroad's brokers and leave it to them to *accumulate* a line at their leisure and at prices *at or around mar-ket levels,* at their leisure, within a certain number of weeks or months if necessary.

The Secret of Success

The way these brokers would go about it would not vary from the conventional methods of accumu-lating, which involves buying, selling, rebuying, re-selling, and buying and selling again. It is a continuous process which aims to get *a long position on balance.*

Herein is the secret, if secret there be, of success for the reader of this little work. If he can detect the buying on balance he will never go far wrong if he operates with a stop loss order, because no matter how many times he may be stopped out, he will eventually be trailing along with the insiders, till the culmination of the operation.

We said before that accumulation and distribution is an expensive matter for the insiders. We are going to use this word unblushingly because of its convenience as designating all those people, persons, and interests who accumulate and distribute securities in a worth-while way. The writer doubts if any more tangible description would apply any better.

A complete accumulative operation taking weeks or months is accompanied by certain very heavy expenses over and above the known commissions, taxes, interest and other carrying charges. Publicity is very expensive and it does not *have* to be bullish publicity in the accumulation stage. The buyer is entitled to a good bargain and cannot be blamed for pointing out the weak points to the seller or the intended seller; and you and I might own the very stock the insider wants to buy. Market operations on a big scale are so very expensive that it takes many points in profits to cover these expenses. Occasionally losses have to be taken; and losses are *expenses* in the life of an insider. He expects to make profits and he knows that he will be wrong very often, and calculates accordingly to cover contingent losses.

Accumulation After a Big Decline

Hence stocks have big, wide swings. This is no accident nor a coincidence. The wide swings ranging ordinarily between 30 to 50 points and more provide a sufficiently big leeway for market interests to accumulate and distribute. They do *not* accumulate their entire line at the bottom as a general rule; they seldom or never distribute (sell out) at or near the top. They are satisfied to conduct their operations around the average prices ruling at the bottom, and to get out within reasonable distance of the top. As one well-known authority and speculator said: "I regard the price range as a yardstick having thirty-six inches. I am satisfied to get twenty-four inches out of the middle."

Accumulation, on the whole, generally takes place near the bottom of a bear market. If, in the typical operation we have spoken of in Reading, the low is 60 and the prevailing price about 65 when accumulation begins, the interests seeking to acquire 50,000 shares on balance would be extremely lucky in securing their stock at an average price between 65 and 70. In a closely held stock like this, the operation would be singularly successful from the accumulating pool's viewpoint.

Pools operating to accumulate a line of stock do not always wait for the bottoms of bear markets *invariably,* as the intervals between the turning points of bear markets are reckoned by years, and not by months. They can decide to accumulate any stock any time, but they would hardly do so excepting after a severe decline of very many points. The instances where this rule has been ignored are so rare as to be classified as exceptions that will not convey a valuable lesson to the student.

CHAPTER II

How to Detect the End of Accumulation

Some Special Points Worth Considering—The Importance of Keeping Records

WHERE the interests seeking to accumulate are not in a hurry, and the depression or bear market is likely to be long drawn out, its wisest course is (and it so instructs its brokers) *not to bid* either actively or aggressively for any stock, but to accumulate stock as it is offered. This is, as the reader will judge, a slow process and results *in extreme dullness and low volume of sales in the coveted issue that gives it an appearance of being lifeless.*

As against a former average activity (turnover) of, we will say, 10,000 to 25,000 shares daily the volume will drop by degrees to 8,000, 5,000, and finally to around 1,000; and on small-volume days where the turnover for the whole market will not exceed around 400,000 to 500,000 shares, the stock under accumulation may show sales of only a few hundred shares.

An Important Point

An important symptom at this time that may be observed is the tendency for the operated stock to break further than the average of the list *on declines,* and to advance less than the average on the *rallies.* This is neither a law nor a rule, but it has been so noticeable in many important accumulative campaigns as to deserve special mention. There is a good reason for this. To accumulate cautiously the brokers in charge or the operator in command of the campaign is compelled to resort to manipulation. This word is not used in any sinister sense; it is merely the science of covering an operator's actions in the stock market. It is often necessary to trade in three, four, or even ten times the quantity of stock the accumulator needs eventually, just as the conjurer in vaudeville in his effort to divert attention from the secret of his tricks resorts to endless chattering, and even pseudo-explanations of how it is done. When the conjurer tells you to watch his right hand carefully, you will naturally learn more if you observe closely his *left hand.*

The pool's aim, or the objective of the big buying interest is to buy cheaply and sell dearly, or retain holdings at a bargain price for investment by the marking down process (applying profits against cost price). To digress a moment to explain this, a certain well-known stock quoted above 100 on the Stock Exchange today is reliably said to have cost the insiders far less than nothing. They have been operating in it for the last ten years very actively, frequently putting it up and down 50 points between the big market swings. If they only make 20 points net every year, they have gained 200 points in the past ten years, and with their stocks quoted at above 100 to-day, it is clear that this is one way of having your pie as well as eating it!

Considering the laudable desire on the part of the buying interests to accumulate as cheaply as possible, no advantage is lost in causing the stock to appear weak at the bottom. This is helped by the apparently thin market (although in reality it is strongest) at the bottom. When volume is small and a further average decline of a point or more in the entire market is recorded in the papers, the appearance of such signs as "-1½," "-2¼," contrasted with "-½" or "-⅜" elswhere in the list, advertises the fact that the stocks that have dropped whole points with fractions to spare are the weakest. They are often *the strongest*.

It is finally noticeable, however, that the stock shows dull strength. In the case of our typical operation in Reading, it will be observed that it swings idly between 65 to 68, dips to 66½ on the next weakness and rises to 69⅜, goes back to 68, and when the first really strong day comes along it crosses 70. It shows that there is little or no stock for sale under 70. The pool has "cleaned up" the floating supply, and has decided to accumulate its next line in the 70s. Meantime it has also sold some stock. The "65 kind" as professional operators speak of their lines has been sold *in part only* at 68, 69 and more, and much of it replaced below 68. While the profits in such incidental trading are substantial and welcome to the average pool (the traffic and turnover being expensive), the primary object being to accumulate, the pool takes care not to lose any stock on balance. We draw the reader's attention to the last six words—an important adjunct in the business of accumulating.

Advancing Volume

When finally, whether it be a month, two months or more before the bear market itself gets out of the rut, or the rails become individually strong or the so-called "coalers" get a move due to forthcoming improvement in that business it will be found that friend Reading is not lacking in a tendency to advance on every occasion that a good excuse can be furnished. These excuses are not necessarily the direct outcome of publicity supplied by the pool in it. The best advertisement a stock can have is— a good rise in it on advancing volume. On such occasion the financial writers, the reporters, the people who supply the financial agencies with news, make it their business to explain the rise. Sometimes they hit the truth; sometimes they analyze the situation very shrewdly. If they are not shrewd, they repeat somebody else's opinion in different words; or by studying the statistics of Reading they discover (mark their deep erudition) that Reading "has an empire of unmined coal expected to be distributed as a melon." If the reader will only analyze this publicity for himself he will find that much of it is of an ancient vintage, yet always welcome to the bull on the stock. Besides, the crop of new speculators and investors is unfailing, and who knows but that they have just discovered that Reading has "got something to do with coal."

A further word as to these ancient and somewhat stale methods. Why does not the public—why do not *you* dear reader—"get onto the fact" that these

same methods serve over and over again, year in
and year out? One would think that big operators,
large interests, manipulators, and pools would change
their tactics, so to speak. They do not—not materially. They have found that these self-same
tactics, the same old rumors, the same story about
a big merger, a melon-cutting, a recapitalization,
and increased dividend whets the public's insatiable,
uninquiring, and greedy appetite, so why bother to
change the method? These methods have worked
with only small variations for fifty years or more,
and even to an extent under the old buttonwood
tree in the last century. This is *one* reason why
the writer believes it possible to help teach the
newcomer by explaining the methods, if the newcomer will but put in the time to assimilate them,
remember them, and act without deviation when the
time comes. These methods may be changed in the
future. Who knows? But we hope to be on the
job at that time to amend, withdraw, or recall anything said to the contrary in this little treatise.

The time comes when the desired "line" of Reading Company has been accumulated in full. Further
purchases would only be made to further the operation; the pool would no longer *go long on balance*.
It would now proceed to sell on balance—to dis-

tribute; and if it felt that at a certain figure, say between 85 and 100, the near-by possibilities will have been "discounted" for a while, you may rest assured that the average pool will not only sell its long stock, but will attempt to secure for itself a substantial short position. It would go short to add to its profits, and to support its market on the following decline.

The reader or student cannot possibly hope to buy at the bottom, remembering that seldom do the insiders accomplish this pleasing performance. If after a long sinking spell with the accompanying dullness our stock swings for weeks and months backward and forward within 10 points of its subsequently known "bottom" (bottom cannot be judged in advance) the accumulating interests will have been lucky to have bought a little stock at the bottom, a little more within 3 to 5 points of the bottom, and the great bulk of their holdings within 10 points. The outsider can often do better than this because his 100, 500, or even 1,000 share purchase can be done openly and he can proclaim it to all the world without attracting a following of a single 100 shares. The insider has but to buy 1,000 shares and "tell the world" before he will find himself paying higher prices for every such indiscretion.

If a record of some kind is kept by the student it will help greatly to "detect accumulation" if such accumulation is on a scale worth while. It is naturally more difficult to discover when the floating supply reaches the millions of shares, as in the big Steel Corporation, and now some of the recapitalized Standard Oils, or Texas Company—all having millions of shares outstanding. Yet this handicap is somewhat overcome by the much wider following such companies have, and the fact that other pools and bullish interests are not slow in taking notice. This will perhaps account for Wall Street's pet expressions "They are *buying*" or "They are *selling,*" as these mythical or actual persons, supposed by the public to be insiders invariably, are in reality the early bulls, acting with or without the first pool or pools, whose business it is to make money in Wall Street by the distribution of stocks to the public. When the second, third or fourth pools are formed on the way up to get their share out of the rise in Reading, or big individual interests, capitalists, millionaire clubmen, wealthy occasional operators, former wealthy connections of the corporations, and their friends begin buying, they form an unassociated "they" that is more powerful than any single inside interest can ever be; and this is the second stage of accumulation that the original pool has been waiting for.

Records Should Be Kept

The big, broad public, consisting of a single individual with $100 to buy 10 shares of Reading on a margin, to the middle western speculator with $1,000,000 to play with, together with the uptown and downtown merchants, the cloak and suit dealers who in the past have consumed a sizeable percentage of the floating supply of stocks in bull markets, the movie magnates, the young millionaire who has just come into the principal of the trust fund of $20,000,000 that the old man made out of a non-adhesive glue—all these people form the composite "they" who will be found on hand to begin nibbling, and finally buying the Reading stock picked up by the original pool, the following pools, the big bulls and finally the little bulls. Substantially before this takes place the accumulation is over, and while trading on the long side will prove profitable until the big interests get out, the turn downward is approaching week by week.

A record of some kind must be kept by the student to observe what is happening. It matters not whether the reader believes in charts, or looks upon those who keep them as a variation of the floating supply of harmless lunatics. It has been the fashion to call the student who keeps such graphic records —a chart-fiend. The chartist doesn't mind what he is called so long as a law is not passed to prevent him from making his mysterious figures and wiggly lines that have no meaning whatever to those who poke fun at or deride his methods.

The record can be kept in mere figures. A small memo book can well contain the daily high, low and last prices, and turnover for each day; or the same record can be kept more conveniently and graphically by means of figure or line charts, samples of which are given elsewhere.

A noticeable flattening out of the drooping branch of lower prices first seen; then some erratic movements that mean little, and finally a well-defined bottom. The picture will finally assume the form of a branch or a growing tree when the sap is rising. Instead of dropping with its own weight, it points firmly up, and if all other conditions are only fair to good, the student can help himself to some of the desired stock.

CHAPTER III

When to Buy and When to Sell

**The Nature of Different Groups in the Market—
Three Classes of Buyers**

IN considering this problem three distinct phases
of the time to buy and sell should be borne in
mind. We have the long pull buyer and seller,
who really takes a semi-investment position, and
seldom need do much in-between trading. This class
of operator, who need not necessarily be in the strict
investment class, would aim to take a position on the
market at the beginning of all the major movements.
He would acquire a line of stocks at or about the
end of a bear market that has run its course, lasting from a year to eighteen months—they seldom
last any longer. One could include in this class,
where he logically "belongs," the "long pull" short
seller, but this type is entirely limited to a mere
handful by comparison. We know of very few (if
any) outside investors or speculators who make a
practice of selling short somewhere near the top, and

staying short until the final termination of the then
current bear market. The buyer at the bottom and
the seller at the top who maintains his position for
months, and on rare occasions for a year or two,
is a variation of the very long pull operator de-
scribed in "A Specialist in Panics," published by *The
Magazine of Wall Street,* an interesting and in-
structive book that the student might well study with
profit.

The second class, which represents the great majority of buyers and sellers, is the big interests, the
pools, the professional operators, the investing and
speculating public, and the kind we can only describe
as the "trailers"—the amateur operators. This class
is in the market when any broad move has already
gotten under way, from a third to half way up a
bull market to the top; it also provides the army that
gets tied up in bull markets; and also provides the
heavy sellers when the market has lost at least a
third of any big advance, and finally in the professional section of this class we find the legion of short-
sellers, mostly of professional or semiprofessional
character. In general, this section of the participating public (which includes the amateur and professional alike) takes part in the buying and selling
during the big rallies and declines preceding the cul-

mination of any current cycle. It needs more skill to participate at this point, but provides the aggregate profits that are worth while. The most active markets are seen at this stage, and next to profits the individual market participant loves activity and *action*.

The third class probably accounts for the largest number of losers in the purely speculative division. As against the minor swings lasting from a month to three months, we have the short swings—the purely technical rallies and declines that punctuate the market in its fairly even course. We will show that in spite of all personal and newspaper talk of "an irregular market," the markets as a whole are uncannily regular most of the time.

The student really wants to know "When to Buy and When to Sell," and we will try to present the advantages and disadvantages of each particular phase in order that the reader may weigh the factors for and against him, and on his capital, training, experience, and temperament decide for himself.

The Long-Pull Method

The long-pull method—buying at the bottom and selling at the top—is probably the ideal one, the most profitable in the long run, and in which the author has seen many of its followers make and retain considerable money, while at all times preserving to the operator a more or less strictly investment attitude. Figures have been published to prove that startling profits have been rolled up by this method of investing (it can hardly be called speculating); by buying the standard high grade securities, particularly some of the gilt-edge rails like New York Central, Union Pacific, Atchison, Southern Pacific, or Chicago Northwestern, all of them dividend payers, all extremely stable, all backed by tangible value that precludes the many elements of danger entering into a purely industrial issue such as obsolescence, competition, duplication, and even mismanagement. These figures not only support the view that it pays the investor and speculator alike to deal in a standard brand of goods like a gilt-edge, dividend-paying rail, but it proves that they are not "slow," not devoid of big swings, and that they have every element of safety combined with large profits.

Without going into unnecessary detail, a consistent long-pull position in some of the leading rails, adding dividends and rights to the original price, and assuming that the holder was able to buy within about 15 per cent of the bottom (surely enough leeway granted even to an amateur), and sold out within 15 per cent of the top, a mere $1,000 grew to between $15,000 to $30,000 in a decade on the average. It takes very little research, and not much in the way of following up consistently earnings and trend for at least twelve months ahead, to be able to take a longer pull position safely. We are aware, of course, of the New Havens, Rock Islands, St. Pauls, Wabashs, and other lame ducks in the railroad division, but the principal losers in these, as any investigation of stock lists proves, have been "the sleeping investors."

Railroads publish their earnings monthly. The net profit can be calculated almost monthly, and it is sufficient to be able to keep track of any corporation (railroad or industrial) in quarterly stages, which is surely not too much for any investor with all the publicity, news agencies, financial magazines, and the financial sections of the leading metropolitan papers devoting such attention to the comings, goings and doings of every corporation. The student will be misled by unjustified optimism, more general statements of insiders, and equally unwarranted pessimism at times. We have known even of deliberate falsehoods, or at least half truths highly colored issued from "official sources" that do occasionally con-

tribute their quota to the investment wrecks, but
the answer to all this is: if an investor or speculator cannot obtain reliable data, facts and figures
and actualities as to the gross business done—
whether he buys a railroad stock or a tire issue—
if he cannot obtain these with fair regularity, and
if they are not in such form to give him an idea
as to whether business is on the up or down grade,
at a profit or loss, then safety will be found in selling out his holdings, and staying out.

The "Top and Bottom"

With these preliminary observations on the big
corporations out of the way, we remind the reader
that money is to be made out of the long-pull method
in standard, gilt-edge stocks by buying them reasonably near the top.   We will commit ourselves by
defining what we mean by "top and bottom."   If an
investor can secure his line within 10 *or* 15 *per cent
of the price* (this does not mean *points*), and can
sell out within a similar percentage of the top, he
is not only accomplishing a lot, but will be doing
that which others have done and profited by immensely.   Remember that Rothschild stated that he
made his money by not trying to buy at the bottom,

and failing to sell at the top. He was probably thinking of that sound idea in investment and speculative practice of trying to get a fair slice out of the middle of the yardstick by which movements are measured. If 36 points or inches represents the yardstick, from 20 to 24 points or inches will be a fair proportion; and we doubt if the best of the greatest known operators ever secured more than this. Certainly the long-pull investors who converted their $1,000 to sums ranging from $15,000 to $30,000 did not *have to* get a bigger proportion.

To answer the first big leading question, "When to buy," the author would counsel the reader to try securing a long position reasonably near the bottom of a bear market that has lasted a year or more; if it hasn't lasted a year or more it has not been a true downswing, and more depression—subject to short rallies of a month or two—is likely.

Another way of judging the time is to look over the yields obtaining in the *very best class of securities*. Take a half dozen or more of the investment issues, common stocks that are paying dividends, and have paid them from five to ten years. Include by all means the Union and Canadian Pacific classes, the U. S. Steels and the Readings, because they are dependable. A motor, film or tire stock might also be paying dividends at the time of this search, and may have been paying them for five years preceding the test. *But it does not mean the same thing.* True the automobile industry is but another phase of the transportation business of the country, but it must be remembered that nearly every railroad in the country "went broke" in the early stages, nearly every standard issue involves new money and assessments put in for reorganization, and one cannot easily duplicate the U. S. Steel's plants and business, nor run an opposition line to the Union Pacific in about less than twenty-five years! In excluding the newer industries like the films, it is not done in any supercilious sense, or because the theater business itself has not become a necessity, but because it has not gone through the crucible of bad times, hard times, panics, depressions, reorganizations, assessments, and then some more assessments. The sound preferred stocks are another important guide, and here also we refer to the most standard kind of which U. S. Steel preferred, American Woolen preferred, Union Pacific preferred, and (yes!) General Motors preferred are all excellent examples. If these preferred stocks begin to show yields that approach 7 per cent on the average, or failing to show that amount of decline, refuse to go down any further despite further breaks in the general list, bad business, and pessimism generally, you can conclude that the bear market has run its course.

At this time (October, 1923) the entire list of common stocks will also show, for those stocks still paying dividends (quite a lot of them will have passed their dividends by that time), handsome yields on the then prevailing purchase price—yields of from 10 to 15 per cent and higher not being uncommon.

The shrewd speculator or investor will then take into account the relative stability of the businesses represented by these depressed common stocks, their dividend record in the past, and average earnings on the common stock for a period of ten years or more. There will be no need at this time to burn the midnight oil too extensvely by studying the whole of Poor's or Moody's Manual. You can get this information on say six of the leading issues with very little trouble. The main point to be sure of is whether there is danger of receivership.

If X, Y and Z stocks show a very large decline from their average quoted price of the preceding five years (not necessarily by comparison with prices of the last bull market), and pay dividends that give an excessive or ridiculous yield compared with the prevailing price for money, you can rest assured that big interests are about ready to withdraw money from enterprises or investments that do not yield as much and go into the good stocks in the stock market—a factor that creates the first stage of stability at low prices and causes the first minor advance at the end of a bear market, and the turn for the next bull market. In the last bear market, for example, Canadian Pacific dropped to around par, and Union Pacific to 110, both with $10 dividends— yielding over 9 per cent. Any tyro knew then, or knows now, that the entire country would have to "go to the dogs" if this were a fair appraisement of Union Pacific. Note also that most other stocks sold at the same ridiculous figures, bearing out the suspicion of a uniform decline where reason and confidence were lost sight of.

Obstacles to Overcome

Loss of confidence and fear are the biggest obstacles to be overcome at such a time; it took courage to buy Union Pacific at 110, and no courage at all to buy it above 150 last year! But the successful speculator must forget his nerves and just follow the dictates of reason to know when to buy for a long pull. Ridiculous yields and only fair earnings with prospect for improvement; dividends mostly maintained and no further general passing of dividends on a wholesale scale (there would be plenty of rumors to the contrary of course); and the average condition of the country reported as fair to improving—away from Wall Street—that is *buying time in good stocks*. It will pay, for the time being at least, not to pay too much attention to the cheap, nondividend paying stocks merely on the theory that they might go up with the rest, until definite reasons (and not surmise) exist for doing the opposite. For example stocks like American Can and Stewart-Warner with their remarkable advances in the last bull market were distinct exceptions to the rule, and complied then as they do now with the exception laid down "until definite reasons exist for doing the opposite." Both then selling around the upper 20s, and certain available in the lower 30s, Can was not paying a dividend, but well able to, by any analysis or test, with (at the time) 2 or 3 times its market price "plowed back" in the seven years preceding its rise. Stewart-Warner had reduced its $4 dividend to $2, but was trailing the automobile prosperity. The Studebaker people had been giving the public a big tip, "This is a Studebaker year," and the action of Studebaker common thoroughly indorsed this claim. Everyone knows now, and might have known then, that Stewart-Warner's speedometers and vacuum tanks were on most standard machines; and its price, earnings, prospects, and undoubted ability to follow up any boom in the auto business was a wide open hint to buy it. It is by such lines of reasoning that other opportunities, quite apart from the high-priced rails, steels, motors, and coppers come along.

The Time to Sell

The time to *sell* in the long pull method, by which we mean the time to get out and stay as reasonable near the top of a bull market is more extensively discussed in a seperate chapter devoted to the subject. More people lose during the final culmination of bull markets (three-fourths of the way up) and at the extreme top than in any other kind, although strange to say that the big distribution does not take place invariable at the top. A rather simple but rough and ready way of judging the top, or reasonably near the top is to watch just a few factors. First, the volume of transactions daily, weekly, and monthly are most important. The number of securities now listed on

the exchanges have doubled and nearly trebled in
the last ten years, and the buying power and in-
crease of interest has grown tremendously since
the Government loan campaigns during the war
created at least a million additional investors and
speculators. While previous ideas on the subject of
volume need revising somewhat so far as proportion is concerned, the big, broad rule holds good.
Beware of going with the mob! Days of 1,000,000
shares or over may continue for weeks, but invariably the market overreaches itself in volume alone,
making it unsafe to go with the crowd. The inflated prices of securities warn unmistakably; trees
never grow to the heavens, yet most people who
lost heavily in bull markets have placed the sky
as the limit in the stocks they hold. When General
Motors sold above $400 a share in the bull market
of 1920, every man in the street "knew" it was
going to $1,000 a share based on the company's
ability to split it up into 10 shares (which it did)
and to boost each unit of the new $10 par stock
—then around $40 to a price of $100. Simple, isn't
it? A look over the list of that time will reveal
exactly opposite conditions to the culminating fea-
tures of buying time at the end of a bear market.
At the top of a bull market, besides the very ob-

viously inflated values, business is superficially booming, everyone is in the stock market (it isn't necessary to include the poor chorus girl and the shoeblack), every body has a tip, and <u>yields are ridiculously *low*</u>. The tendency of the market to *anticipate* if properly looked into will reveal that few corporations are in a position to increase their dividends beyond the dividend disbursements being paid when stocks sell very high; and only increased earnings plus increased dividends that can safely be disubrsed can further boost prices. Recapitalizations, mergers, melons, rights, are as plentiful as flies in June at such a time, and it is selling time under the long-pull method.

Other periods comprise the minor swings, over a period ranging from months to weeks—swings that last a few days are those brought about by the technical position only, due to short covering, further short selling and the evening up of the business of professionals. The minor swings are usually accompanied by a fair degree of activity, and a daily volume that at the present time would average from 500,000 to 800,000 shares daily.

The first break in a bull market is usually a severe one, and continues for one, two, or even three months until the many speculative bulls are eliminated, and a large short interest created—such short interest being almost solely of a professional character, and also helped by the short selling of the former bull pools who have sold out in the previous bull market, and have gone short to protect their stocks, and make further money on the down side. Usually a state of dullness is reached after a quarter to one-third the entire previous advance is lost, and while the reaction has calmed down the hysteria somewhat, hope still exists and confidence has not yet been entirely shattered. The high prices brought about in the previous bull market are still remembered and much unwise buying is brought in as a consequence. It is safe under such conditions not to "buck the advance," but to follow up both the activity in selected good stocks based on increasing daily volume in them, as well as steady volume on the upgrade in the market in general. It is safe, if not essential, to use stop loss orders, because in following up such a rally in what may turn out to be a fairly long bear market, it is difficult to judge the time or extent of the next downswing, and one can only hope to get a bit out of the middle in all subsequent rallies. Short selling is not yet advisable because the pools still have their stocks well in hand, the pools themselves are probably short and know more about it than the outside trader, and the public is still willing to follow up the rallies and make a short position uncomfortable.

Deceptive Conditions

It will be noted at this time that not all stocks go up nor rally vigorously. Very often former leaders remain almost stationary, or rally feebly, while new leaders are brought out and made to appear strong in order to engender the feeling that the bull market is still existent. Such new leaders can be "played" on the activity as it develops. These should be protected by stop loss orders. Many skilled speculators and professional traders sometimes hedge their long position in new leaders by going short of the former leaders that rally feebly, or refuse to go with the stocks that are now being made strong to cover a retreat or distribution in others. This is not, generally speaking, a good time to buy securities on their merits for income, for the best stocks will either advance very little, or be procurable in the next bear market at lower prices. This is not a hard and fast rule, however. Sometimes sheer merit will overcome all obstacles, and a special group will begin to complete an ad-

justment actually begun in the previous bull market.
If this be due to special trade influences it will pay
to follow *the group;* to select the best in the group
being "bulled," on the ground that powerful interests contemplate some special move which may not
be as successful as if begun in the bull market
proper, but still affording sufficient action and profit
to justify "following through." A notable example
of this is seen in the action of the chain-store issues
in the 1922-1923 bull market. Woolworth, Kresge,
and even some of the mail-order concerns like Sears-
Roebuck were late in responding to the better business conditions that set in from the beginning of
1922; the student need entertain no suspicion of
the genuineness of the move if investigation proves
higher prices justified. We would not follow up
every stock in a group because the leaders in it
have gone up, although it might pay to do so in
the second class issues for a fair profit if the commitment be protected with a stop loss order.

Selling for the decline on the secondary reaction
down to the next plane of prices is the point where
the insiders sell largely. Distribution is largely
accomplished at that point. The public likes to buy
stocks that have declined from extremely high prices,
a form of securing supposed bargains. The bull

who has overstayed his bull market also buys there
"to average down." It is a good place to sell as a
rule, because the next reaction will ordinarily be
far more severe and go further than the first stop.
Again, assuming the operator protects himself with
a stop loss order, he can do as many professional
operators do—sell a fair quantity, intending that
one-half his sales he will stand by to the end of
the long downswing, and that he will cover when
liquidation on a big scale (indicated by increasing
volume on the downside) has run its course. This
may take from a month to six weeks or more, but
the end will come with extreme dullness, and the
general public entirely out of te market. Generally a
piece of disturbing news, whether at home or abroad,
will be seized upon as the last excuse to cause a heavy
volume of sales, forced sales through margin calls,
and perhaps another day or two of the cleaning-up
process and more margin calls. A day of confusion
will come that is unmistakably discouraging to any
bull, and on that day again we would cover short contracts and buy for a rally. It might be safe to wait
a day or two for confirmation of our opinion, *but a
venture may always be made with a stop loss order
placed 2 points or so below the low prices reached*
in the entire move on the day of heaviest volume.

CHAPTER IV

How to Analyze Market Swings

Difference Between Railroad and Industrial Securities

THE analysis of market swings is largely a matter of proper appraisement of the momentum of stocks; and we may say in general that it applies to the market as a whole as well as to individual stocks. The man who is a good judge of the market as a whole will be found shrewdly correct on the average so far as individual securities are concerned. Because of the special influences in particular stocks, their degree of capitalization, their earnings, dividends and the possibility of continuance, discontinuance, or increasing on facts unknown to the outside world, it is more profitable to study the market as a whole, or at most a group of stocks based on their classification and importance, and from thence apply the principles learned to individual issues.

The reader may, or may not know, that experts

do not always speak of Sinclair being weak, Reading being strong, or Republic remaining stationary. There is a wide difference in the swings between the two big classifications of *rail and industrials*. It is not within our province to go into all the elements that have made this broad distinction, but suffice it to mention here that railroads have always held a more permanent niche in the investment field because, for example, promoters do not in these days attempt to "fleet a railroad" over night; their investment capital has reached enormous proportions in every case, and it would be rather difficult for new interests to start a new railroad. Railroads are as permanent as downtown New York skyscrapers; the output is now decidedly limited, and except for branch lines to existing roads, and perhaps much double and even quadruple tracking in time, the wants of the nation are fairly well supplied.

Besides, $50,000,000 or even $100,000,000 cuts no real ice in the railroad business, whereas a small part of that sum will be sufficient to start a prosperous ice and coal business for example (this is not an intentional pun). A business can depend on a single person's personality, and an old business can be bought up to-day, new funds put in next month, and the whole system revamped in a year.

Then, again, let someone build up a business that is successful, whether it be in tires, shoes, automobiles, or even raw material such as paper or hides; next year, if such business is successful this year, a number of (more or less) shoestring concerns can begin to compete. This factor is present, the danger is there, and the staggering number of commercial failures—year in and year out—as reported by Dun's and Bradstreet's, finds not a single man or firm failing through trying to begin a new railroad. It simply isn't done.

Various Types of Industrials

Thus we find a broad line of demarcation between the so-called issues, ranging from the big Steel Corporation down to the latest genius (or near genius) in the merchandising of coffee, ham or tea. Some of these become successful in a national way like Woolworth with his 5s and 10s (the stock at $250 a share!), others go to the wall like Clarence Saunders with his Piggly-Wiggly. Success in an industry is judged in Wall Street by the result; there is no sympathy, no hurrahing on the way uphill; on the contrary, the cynical short-seller and the pessimist on values is ever present as he was fifty years or more ago. The industrials have their own groups, and in those groups their own "class."

The third big group is the public utility, the tremendous national enterprises, so called because they cater to the essential living needs of 110,000,000 people, from the cradle upward in the way of life-giving heat, machine-driving power, essential light, transportation, and communication by telephone, to say nothing of gas for every purpose, natural gas in the communities where this is abundant, oil for heating, light and power, and a hundred things that the community finds so essential as to create the corporations that come under the supervision of Public Service Commissions, Interstate Commissions, and the Government itself. Their immense investments in power and service lines, out of all proportion seemingly to the visible and invisible comforts provided, and the small tax on the individual member of the community for that service, endow the public utility with a sanctity and virtue all its own, that has appealed—even on sentimental grounds —to the investor throughout the land.

Securities Do Not All Advance at Once

So, in speaking of market swings, despite the presence of all kinds of securities, the three major branches like railroads, industrials and public utilities, they do not all "swing" in the same direction at the same time. When business is bad, money not wanted because purchases are light, money is offered at very low rates, causing advances in (firstly) good bonds, (secondly) medium bonds, (thirdly) preferred stocks, and (lastly) common stocks—the good investment stocks. The war markets, for example, years of intense speculation, years of "easy money," sees the investment stocks not wanted because big dividends in more speculative common stocks, and their ability to run the whole gamut of emotional excitement up and down the speculative scale—these things draw the money away from the rails and public utilities. A big speculative industrial market will either see a declining rail and public utility market or no action in them. During the entire war-boom public utilities and rails sank to the vanishing point.

In considering market swings, therefore, the student and reader must draw a sharp distinction between the three big divisions in the stock market, and then proceed to watch the industrial market by its own groups because this market is so huge, so broad, so comprehensive in its scope that it is not possible to watch the whole, nor to judge well except by reference to the whole.

There are certain groups and certain stocks in these groups that will always, generally, furnish the best analysis of the swing itself. Suppose, for example, a big rise in the automobile stocks is witnessed against a stationary or declining market in the steels. Now an automobile stock might be a good temporary "leader" if it is actually the recognized leader in its group. A rise of Mack Truck or Moon Motors might mean nothing to the group if Studebaker and General Motors is declining. But if the rise begins with General Motors (rather out of "leadership" honors through recapitalization) and is taken up by Studebaker, and White Motors, Mack Trucks, Moon Motors, Hudson Motors, Packard and the rest follow, we are justified in analyzing that swing as having especial significance for the automobile group—but we are not justified in saying "This is a bull market."

Temporary Market Leaders

Leadership shifts around. Railroads were in former years the real leaders, and when they began moving they attracted the best investment interests throughout the country. It is possible they might be restored to some of the favor they formerly held; a new generation has forgotten the disappointments of years ago; but their real leaders, like Union Pacific, Southern Pacific, Atchison, New York Central, have displaced the old time Lackawanna, Delaware & Hudson and Chicago Northwestern, to say nothing of Northern Pacific that attained a figure of $1,000 a share in its time. The rails are *good* leaders despite their fall from grace, because it takes "real money" to build a bull market in the railroads. However, in recent years the railroads have had many false starts, due perhaps to fear of strikes and higher wages on the one hand and unfavorable legislation on the other hand. As this is written, a good deal of interest is being injected into the railroad group again, and if the author be allowed the luxury of a single forecast, it is not unreasonable to suppose that they have "come back" for good in the last three years, and the prosperity of many old time plodders like New York Central and Baltimore & Ohio provides a basis of new leadership in many railroads in widely different groups like the coalers, the grangers, the Southwestern group, and the fairly prosperous Pacific group. They provide such a vast variety in such widely different fields as to constitute, in their own somewhat limited sphere, an almost different type of industry analogous to the oil stocks that represents a gasoline merchant, and the public utility that is really an oil company.

Not a Difficult Problem

It is not a difficult matter to analyze major swings, so long as the student will not attempt to explain to himself the day-to-day movements—the wheels within wheels that really depend on the big motive force, the flywheel that is operating the works. The best way to explain a thing is often to show it, and demonstrate its practical workings. We refer the reader to the graphic record of the industrial group of stocks since 1897. It will be noted in the first place that the tendency of industry has been upward, and that we must continually look for bull markets and bear markets with fairly well distributed regularity.

In analyzing a "swing" we again cannot escape the factor of volume—inextricably bound up with the movement. The top of a movement is shown, perhaps not at the moment (because volume next day may be still larger) by a volume often out of proportion to the rise. The 1901 "top," for example, was not materially above the 1899 top, yet the participants, operators, the public interest was at fever heat with a volume above 40,000,000 shares in a single month. Had *buying* predominated in the summer of 1901, in other words had the excess demand for around 30,000,000 shares been the result of natural demand (compare this volume with that of midsummer of 1899—around 10,000,000 shares), the rise should not have stopped far short of 85 to 90, or at least a 50 per cent gain in the averages. The months following witnessing a dramatic sudden fall showed that the outside public were not entirely shaken out—the volume dropped radically. In 1902 powerful interests made a second attempt to interest a bullish following without success, and the terrific fall of 1903 was a direct sequel to these events.

An Important Signal

Attention is drawn to a valuable "signal" that occurs very often in the foothills of a bear market. The beginning of the 1904 rise is marked by some obvious supporting points. By early spring the volume of sales began to rise—prices following the activity, showing there was little stock for sale at those figures. The greatly increased volume in summer and onward, and the "step by step" action of

the market following leading to the rampant bull
markets of 1905-1906 is a market swing that is
unmistakable.

One can often detect coming market swings of
this character by simple observation and "putting
two and two together." The student of that time
could hardly have mistaken the 1904 market, even
in the beginning or early stages. The drastic fall
of 1903, relative steadiness in the bear market,
diminishing volume, dullness, followed by steady
upward moves (small at times it is true), is a good
example for the student of momentum. When the
biggest move of all took place in the early summer
of 1904, shown clearly by "the longest leg" all
above the range of the market of the previous ten
months, only one analysis was possible—the turn
has come.

We refer the reader to the top of 1909, when for
nearly a full half year securities remained within
a five-point range, which ended with a precipitate
smash of 8 points in a single month. Does the
volume tell us anything here? It is not a clear
guide on this occasion, it must be admitted, although
the average ranged above 20,000,000 shares monthly
—abnormal in those times, which coupled with the
narrow range following what everyone should have

known was—a bull market, little excuse here existed
for staying long at the top, and failing to take
advantage of the opportunity to sell short that followed.

Coming down to more recent markets, the student
will not fail to understand the lesson of the big
war market culminating in the fall of 1919. The
volume of trading itself reached the highest monthly
record in fourteen years. Preceding the peak month
of November came a year of such intensive activity
as markets have seldom or ever seen. Little wonder
that this month called for a reprimand from high
banking quarters—the Federal Reserve authorities.
We think that nothing but hysteria called for the
high prices then prevailing—keen analysis becomes
a light task under such conditions.

The reverse swings from bear markets upward
are as simple in their fundamentals. It is as well
to watch suspiciously declining volume. Note, for
example, the beginning of 1904 and the disorganized
market beginning 1915. It is all a matter of proportion judged by the work of the preceding months
and years.

Our markets have been immensely broadened in
the last few years; there are more stocks, more corporations, more public. The population has in-

creased; likewise the supply of speculators and investors. But despite the greater handicap calling for more careful comparison, the examples given may well form a basis for further research and comparison that we believe will not be unproductive in conjunction with your further labors in this field.

CHAPTER V

How to Gauge the Technical Position

Force As the Principal Element in the Market

IN this chapter of our studies of the market we arrive at a milestone which marks the real junction of all turning points; the conclusion reached by every individual, large or small, who by his willingness to buy or his eagerness to sell stamps the market with a sold out position, an overbought position, or one of waiting for the next development. At the latter stage it is likely to rally or decline again, but the probability is always in favor of the character of the general market—more eager to rally in a bull market, and ready to stage a further decline in a bear market.

Let us understand clearly what is meant by technical position. It is worth getting a clear perception of the subject because no other factor, single or combined, is as important to success in the market as understanding the technical position, and working in harmony with it.

The market goes up or down according to the number, type and dollar value of buyers and sellers. It is a study in "stresses" so well known to tne engineer, and can be calculated almost as readily and with a degree of mathematical precision that is surprising. It is on this study, and the ability to summarize such studies into rapid advice and action, that the market expert is able to forecast future movements with a large percentage of accuracy. Whether the expert is consciously a mathematician, or an engineer, or is relying upon the well-organized "sixth sense"—his feel of the market—his intuition, all of which undoubtedly come to the man who has made a very long, close, earnest and scientific study of stock prices and movements, back of it all is his ability to logically explain to himself just why stocks should go up one day and decline violently the next.

It is entirely impossible in a brief work of this kind to more than scratch the surface of this absorbing and all important subject. We hope for the sake of presenting the student of the future with a valuable record of experiences it may be possible to devote a whole book to the subject some day. Meanwhile we can explain some phases of technical position that may well be a starting point to the reader for his further observation and study.

Balance Between Supply and Demand

Technical position is then nothing else but a crystallization of the balance between supply and demand. To put the matter quite crudely, and perhaps in valuable vivid form to our readers, we asked a very experienced veteran trader who has (really and truly) made an honest-to-goodness fortune in the market, kept it, and still trades just to keep himself employed. We asked him one day during weeks of reaction after reaction, just by way of satisfying our own curiosity, and perhaps confirming our belief, "What's the matter with this market, Mr. ——?" He just grinned, shrugged his shoulders and said, "Oh, nothing much—*just more sellers than buyers!*" The judge or observer of technical conditions does not concern himself with the why and wherefore of the market's going up or down; he doesn't argue with the market; he does not "buck the trend" (bulling a bear market or the reverse); he doesn't take comfort from optimistic publicity when stocks go down, or console himself with pessimistic utterances when it continues to go up while he has sold out. Not at all. He studies and takes notice of the fact that a market will persist in going up while every published report is gloomy, and all

the news of the day and week is bad; a strong market in the face of "bad news" (a general term meaning pessimistic conditions). He says to himself:
"A strong technical condition; more buyers than
sellers—trend still upward until for the time being
the condition is reversed—why or how I do not
care." The student who will trouble himself to find
reason for every nonexplainable advance or decline
either in the whole market or individual issues will
spend his time in vain. The Steel Corporation (we
like quoting this big fellow) has about 5,000,000
shares outstanding owned by every class of individual, male and female, big, little and medium;
clerk, shoemaker, employee and capitalist. You cannot get them to think alike consecutively for longer
than a day or two at most (*if* they ever think alike).
The specialists in Steel, as well as in every stock
like to stabilize their securities against extreme advances or declines. They have supporting orders all
the time, very often orders against extreme advances
or declines. They have always scale orders to *sell,*
not only for profit purposes, and for liquidation,
but also to stabilize securities on the upside. Amer-
ica is foremost in maintaining a broad open market
or remarkably stable values considering the enor-

mous floating supply of securities and the flood of new emissions every year.

But supply and demand is not a thing that can be regulated. Fortunately it can be interpreted; we will not claim with mechanical exactitude, nor consistently week in and week out. There is no infallibility in market judgment or the science of forecasting (and *science it is*) because of the impossibility of judging accurately even the effect of the weather on the courage and mood of the buying and selling public. Naturally rosy conditions and the prospect of their continuance keeps people in a bullish mood; they buy. When the realization is attained and all have money, they buy again, and the number of buyers is increased—sometimes the price doesn't matter. Witness the shoe dealer who during the war-boom offered for sale identical shoes at $9 and $12 and could sell only the $12 kind. The technical position is the buying and selling conditions—the balance between supply and demand, sometimes controlled largely by the public (a runaway market is that kind), and sometimes partly by the public and partly by professional operators. This period is during the halfway and concluding stages of a bull market. The higher stocks go up the more dangerous they become, because earnings and dividends will support prices just "so far" and no more. Every stock has a limited value for the time being, based on dividend prospects or its dividend at this time, and the possibility of an increase. The return on money is largely the guiding factors, and stocks try to adjust themselves to the existing money rates a few months ahead.

The Question of Dividends

All the news received by the public, the pools, the insiders, or anyone else resolves itself into a single question in the end. How much in dividends will Whatsthis or Whosthat pay now, next year and the year after in consequence ·of the present news, its earnings and the earnings of the future. The technical position is constantly trying to adjust itself to present values, and *present* values take into account a good deal of the intangible future. A stock can have no great "tangible" value and yet sell high, while stocks with a high "tangible" value can sell for a mere song. Their prices are based on their present and future ability "to deliver the goods" in the way of dividends and income to future holders. Once the value is definitly known, for example, guaranteed stocks and Government bonds, they will cease to fluctuate daily, weekly or even monthly, and move solely on their income yield aligned with yields prevailing on commodities of a similar kind at that time.

You will find daily statements in newspapers, brokers' letters and market literature "the market declined for technical reasons only," or "the technical position is strong," or the reverse. It means simply, as our humorous veteran friend said, "There were more buyers than sellers," therefore the market went up. Just *why* there should be more, better, and stronger buyers to-day than yesterday may be due to very many reasons; good news, an oversold condition, a big short interest driven to cover through a bullish development in the news, a restored dividend in an important stock of an important group, or even (take this seriously please) better weather conditions.

The seasonal fluctuations in the market form an interesting commentary on the temperamental side of human nature, quite apart from the influence of seasons on business. The summer is often dull in the stock market, yet the corn is ripening, the crops are maturing, the railroads are running full tilt, people are burning up the roads and gas in their cars, using up oil—but they do not feel energetic enough to desire to make money. In the spring we often have "the spring rise" explained (not wholly facetiously) because the sap is rising up the trees, and man awakens from his long winter indoors and looks forward with exhilaration and pleasure to the pleasant days to come. The investor and speculator feels "good" then; he is able to take his courage in both hands and take a chance. The fall activity in the stock market (often down as well as up, but nearly always active) is due to the energetic season when people take stock of themselves and their belongings. In the fall they either sell heavily or buy heavily; they are likely to think of quantity production or quantity liquidation, and we usually get active markets, one way or other in the fall. The motor shows are always well advertised in the beginning of the year; people see cars, read about them and order them; their mind is on motor stocks, and they usually buy if they consider themselves able to pick bargains. In the spring again mining is usually active; the textile and woolen business is active; the mills are running full speed; here again thoughts turn naturally to the securities of the companies active at that time.

We need not concern ourselves too seriously, for speculative purposes at least, touching the reasons that create good and bad technical positions so long as we recognize the predominating influence of the presence and action of buyers, or their absence. We can translate these studies into actual facts and figures by recognized methods that are used, studied and followed by market judges and students.

Let us consider the graphic record of market movements covering a period of twelve sessions, and see whether we cannot deduce from the technical position *alone* without reference to the names of the stocks, the volume of sales, nor even the period of operation, a logical and reasonable interpretation of the probable direction of the next move. We can apply this reasoning almost all along the line. The legend below the graph is sufficiently explanatory, but the author will ask the reader merely to note the closing prices as indicated by crosses, and to follow a technical analysis of the movement.

1. Starting point; close was lowest; technical position weak.
2. A drop of nearly 5 points, slight recovery at close; still weak.
3. An excellent recovery with close at top; sudden reversal indicates a possible shakeout or special liquidation has occurred.
4. Opinion confirmed here; all lost ground

recovered, and close is maintained near top.

5. Only confirms 3 and 4.

6. A reaction due entirely to *technical condition;* recovery evidently too rapid. The close near bottom looks like a good piece of advertising to sell. Would rather stay long.

7. Same, a further decline without yielding a full point further.

8. Opening within a half point range, followed by a session of immense strength. Stay long.

9. Further confirmation of 3, 4, 5 and 8, strengthened by day's lowest price materially above lowest price in *four* days. Obviously more buyers than sellers.

10. No stock pressing for sale; holders and buyers not tempted, although advance slowed up. Close is at top for third time. Technical position excellent.

11. Further confirmation of all the foregoing, and "new high territory" reached.

12. The big rise has induced no important selling or the close would not be in such dangerous ground to shorts and possible sellers.

This little analysis could be extended by reference to the volume of sales, which would also further elucidate the position. If, for example, the volume increases on the decline we can usually deduce that inasmuch as, numerically, sellers exceed buyers as indicated by the number of shares sold the technical position is weak, and will contiue weak until the selling pressure is removed as shown by diminishing volume. When the volume becomes subnormal—judged by comparison with average sales for days preceding—the technical position has reached a state of flux or balance. We just have to watch again for the direction of the movement in bigger volume, *that is all!* It stands to reason that, if after a period of dullness following heavy liquidation on the downside we pass to dullness, no transactions worth while (therefore no selling pressure *in volume*) the supply at that time has petered out. If then the market moves up, or an individual stock we may be watching does the same, we are justified in concluding at least that the pressure being off, the lid lifted, the tendency is towards normal—which is probably higher than the extreme depression point for that period. If coupled with a moderate rise the volume increases likewise, the movement has only one way to go—upward.

When an individual stock or the market as a

whole has advanced or declined extensively we are always confronted with a weakened or strengthened technical position—invariably. A stock has a fixed value. It can stand so much in the way of value based on many factors. People will continue to buy it until a price is reached where it is no longer attractive, either to insiders, pools, manipulators or the veriest tyro. Just as a piece of strong copper wire can be stretched and stretched again and perhaps not break even though put to severe strain, its tensile strength becomes weakened as the stretching process proceeds. A stock, or the market for that matter, will change hands at ever advancing prices, subject only to minor reactions (due solely to the technical position) until the succeeding buyer or groups of buyers are weaker and less competent judges of the market or securities. The good judge does not wait to buy on top of a 50-point rise. The weakest buyers and holders are invariably near the top. The stock or the market gets into weak hands as prices go up, and still weaker as the technical position gets more crucial, as short selling by stronger professional interests proceeds, and these professionals are using all their arts and wiles to "pound" both the stock and the market for the purpose of

entrenching their own short position, and later covering for profit.

The volume of sales is another good index of the
technical position. The technical position is strongest at the bottom and weakest at the top because
insiders are in command at low prices, and outsiders
"carry the bag" during a time of price inflation.
When transactions are small, volume is normal, and
prices are reasonable, securities are either lodged
with investors, institutions, banking interests, or so-
called insiders, or they are immune from big price
swings becaues the holders are seldom or ever neces-
sitous sellers.

Volume of Sales as an Index

As the volume of sales rises, the price also goes
up, whether in the average as a whole or in stocks
in particular. So long as the prices as a whole go up
with volume of transactions, the market is a per-
fectly natural one, because more buyers with more
money are on hand to assert higher values with actual cash. But the time comes when *volume out-
strips movement;* when the volume remains high
and even increases, but the market as a whole,
as judged by the averages, does not make progress
rateably with the volume of sales, that indicates dis-

tribution coming into the market, and the technical position becoming weaker. In number, buyers may still exceed sellers, but the *quality* of the buying, and its importance may be bad, or uninformed. Individual stocks may still be going up; specialties and pool issues under expert control stage individual movements which are not an index of the technical position. *The thing to watch is the averages as a whole, balanced against the volume as a whole.*

Regarding market averages, a few comments are necessary. Many kinds of averages are kept by various institutions, financial agencies, advisory bureaus and newspapers. The *N. Y. Times* and the Dow-Jones averages are, on the whole, the most generally followed. They are not by any means ideal, because they include too many nonrepresentative issues. Any compilation of averages is apt to be too long employed, and too arbitrarily referred to without reference to quickly changing conditions, such as unimportance of certain industries; faulty balance of individual security prices against others. due to exceptional or unforeseen causes; changes of capitalization, making comparisons almost impossible, and other elements too technical to be discussed at length. Still, the published newspaper averages are extremely valuable to the student, and he can form a good idea of the price curves by subscribing to a few good financial papers and keeping on file for reference the averages as a whole. The *N. Y. Times* gives composite figures which the student may form into graphs of 25 leading railroad stocks, 25 industrial issues, and a "combined" figure arrived at by using the entire 50 stocks just mentioned. The result is shown in three different curves known as the industrial averages. This, road averages and the combined averages. This, together with the daily information as to number of shares handled each day on the New York Stock Exchange (sufficiently representative of the entire country) will enable the reader to have a picture of what is really doing in the market. This is a better procedure than the unfortunate method employed by thousands who buy or sell 100 shares of this or 500 shares of that, and look in the evening or morning paper to see whether their particular stock has gone up five points or dropped an eighth! Better to follow these averages than to see what the bright young reporter thinks of the market, or why (according to his version) American Sugar went down two points and U. S. Rubber went up one point.

What Makes Market Conditions

The movement of the entire market is closely
bound up with fundamental conditions; in part the
stock market moves help to *make conditions*. When
stocks are high, banks lend a pile of money on them.
Let the "averages" drop five points and 1,000,000
shares be sold out, the banks receive funds, loans are
called, and the further loaning value of the balance
is reduced. Bull markets create countrywide optimism; in their wake is prosperity and courage. Business development goes ahead or is planned mostly in
bull markets. There is usually full employment then.
The averages translate all this for you.

Statistics and corporation reports, as well as trade
reports in particular industries, are a guide when
stocks are low and somewhat of a clue to their technical position. If stocks are depressed after heavy
and long drawn out liquidation, their technical position is likely to be strong. If they are apparently
"weak" and neglected in the market, the first weeks
of rising prices on increased volume is an indication
that they have become a purchase rather than a sale.
The technical position gets weaker as good news is
about to be published, not invariably but very often,
on the theory that earlier informed people have long

since taken proper and adequate action to buy early
and sell out the moment "the novelty of the good
news wears off." Conversely the news as to the
passing of a dividend, long expected to be passed
or discounted in falling prices, creates a stronger
technical position if only for the reason that selling
will shrink since the further probability of substantial profit becomes offset by the risk of continuing
to stay short.

The technical position is not *always* improved by
a continuous decline either in the market or an individual stock. A decline weakens confidence, and
when a stock or the market declines too far it creates a semipanicky condition in that stock based
on the assumption that there is excellent reason, not
always disclosed, at the time of the decline. Very
often a stock will continue to show continued selling
pressure for no apparent reason; but the reason is
there you may be assured, and it is well to stay out,
and even to go short (with a stop loss order), preferring to follow the movement in its chosen but
not always explained direction, rather than to take
a mere chance or make a mere guess that because
the stock is very low it *must* be cheap. That is not
an argument for buying. Conversely, an unexplained advance, followed by consistent strength,

and persistent advances for unexplained reasons is usually the result of forthcoming development of a favorable nature not yet published. The quiet, unheralded advances in small volume take place usually under a good technical condition of a stock, not widely held, not widely tipped, and usually able to follow its own chosen path of least resistance. The technical position usually discloses itself by the resistance a stock shows to selling on the way up, and its refusal to stay supported on the way down. Millions of shares outstanding in any issue are a strong factor in a decline where buyers are in a timid mood, and the technical position will not become strong until a thoroughly sold out condition is reached, and the stock becomes cheap in the opinion of people better informed than the general public. Issues of small capitalization are often not so able to maintain as stable a technical position as stocks whose capitalization inclines to the 1,000,000 or more shares held by the public. Naturally their market is not as broad, and on the way down are likely to break quite violently between sales during highly nervous sessions due to the absence of rhythmic support; that is to say, buyers on the way down at fractions of points. The specialist or the insider is not a wizard. The human factor is always present in stock trading. The insider cannot always guess correctly and his orders to buy on a scale down are sometimes withdrawn, or even overlooked until support becomes essential.

By studying the averages continuously and judging price movements as a whole, by noting the volume of sales not only in individual issues but in the whole market, by noting the extent of the movement contrasted with the number of shares per movement, the student should gain an insight into judging the technical position, which as a factor is more important than any others combined.

CHAPTER VI

How to Detect Turning Points

IN a rather broad way the detection of turning points follows certain stock market fundamentals, with variations to allow for the changing character of the style, breadth, volume, trend of speculation and investment, methods of operators, popularity of stocks and industries, and a multitude of other elements that follow no given set of conditions from year to year.

In speaking of turning points there are many "turns" to be considered. We have the long pull or minor cycle running from the bottom of a bear market to the top of a bull market, a period that varies, but in recent years may be roughly estimated as follows:

Approx. Years

1897-1899—a bull market.................. 3
1900—almost entirely a bear market with last
  two months strong rally................. 1
1901-2—bull market interrupted by Northern
  Pacific panic (brief), with heavy distribution

Approx. Years

in 1902 .... **2**

1903—a violent bear market, undigested securities panic 1

1904-1905-1906—one of the greatest bull markets in American history 2½

1907—Money panic; bear market of great vio-
lence 1

1908-1909—bull market 2

1910-1911—bear market 2

1912—bull market 1

1913-1914—bear market 2

1915-1916—bull market 2

1917—bear market 1

1918-1919—bull market, the last year of which
made a record in market history........... 2

1920-1921—bear market 2

1922—bull market 1

1923—bear market (to September).......... 1

It will be seen that the duration of each market
varies. On the whole bear markets *have been*
shorter than bull markets, averaging about one year
as against an average of twice that time for bull
markets. The above one and two year periods we,
for the purpose of continuing, consider the main

swings of the market, running from one to three years. A complete market cycle runs from bottom of one bear market to the bottom of the next. Some statisticians profess to see periods of from ten to twenty-five years between "cycles." Life is short and it will not pay the reader to worry about more than two of these great cycles at most. Let us then consider the three year cycles and the near-by future which we can live, enjoy, and by which we may profit.

Duration of Markets

The real turning points occur at the top of bull markets and at the bottom of bear markets. Because of this fact some statisticians claim that action is invariably followed by reaction, as in mechanical laws. It has been attempted to disprove this theory; it is claimed that the "business curve" of extreme prosperity down to depression, unemployment, bear markets and other accessories can be "flattened out." The sooner this comes the better, of course, but to deny the theory and ridicule it is to emulate the Kentucky Colonel, look at the cold figures, see the terrific swings since 1897 and say "There is no sich animal as bull and bear markets; there's no manipulation; no turns—and there ain't going to be any in the future." Some Utopian plan may be worked out by the supermen of the coming generations, we have no doubt. Meantime we have to content ourselves with the precedents of American economic history over the past hundred years, particularly as it affects the securities markets. We feel that good opportunities to detect turning points will come, and in their detection many of our present readers perhaps trying to understand the markets for the first time will look back to the present observations herein recorded, and agree (more or less) with the author. So far as we can see ahead, human nature will not alter. The American temperament leans towards taking a chance, which is to *speculate* or "invest enthusiastically," and the result creates the wide swings.

Every bull market must run its course and every bear market must uncover bargains—stocks paying dividends selling at ridiculous levels. The obvious invitation is: get something for nothing (or nearly so) by selling when stocks are too high, or buying when they are too low.

The turn at the end of the minor cycle is not obvious nor even possible to detect with any great degree of accuracy *at the moment of occurrence*. Subsequent action is needed to confirm an opinion, no matter how well founded or informed. Without subsequent action, such as continued weakness and lower averages at the top, or continued buying with *higher* averages at the bottom; these usually come soon enough to enable one who is long to protect himself, the shorts to cover near the bottom.

At the top or near the bottom of a bull market the daily and weekly turnover reaches enormous proportions and for a time new high records in the averages are hung up daily.

Large Turnovers

New stocks are taken up, new groups, new favorites, and often the groups dominated by certain favorite pools, manipulators and market leaders— men whose names are on every tongue. Everybody you meet holds stocks; there isn't standing room in the board rooms of brokers' offices; everybody seems to be making money (running up and pyramiding paper profits), tips are gratis and numerous. New dividends are declared and old passed dividends are resumed. The smash is really "just around the corner," but the atmosphere breathes confidence and excitement; the high market finds most people *with money to buy at the top* (no one has money in a bear market). One cannot blame investors, big interests, pools, speculators, and insiders for wishing to sell "while the selling is good."

The selling is easiest while the public is in control, as attested by the large volume and ridiculous prices; and the selling takes place *right there* and on the way down. Sometimes certain stocks are taken up and advanced beyond all reason—hundreds of points rise in individual stocks or those in a special group is not uncommon. If it took so many years for a stock to find out that it was worth 200 to 500 as against less than 100 in five previous years, is it not time for the speculator and investor to do a little thinking? Is it not a proper inference that where half a dozen values are highly exaggerated there is a suspicion that there is exaggeration all along the line. *Of course!* The time comes rapidly when it will be noted that while some stocks are doing "their stuff"—advancing rapidly while others are either stationary or giving ground, it will be carefully explained that switching is taking place, thus accounting for Whatsthis Steel or Whosthat Oil failing to continue its advance. Nothing of the kind. The real owners of W. Steel and W. Oil have not become millionaires by following the crowds; they are not only probably out of their stocks, but a fair percentage of them—of course the more speculative among them—have already taken a short position.

The turn comes when the public is in control, when volume is abnormally high, when values are unreasonably and too rapidly advanced, when the averages as a whole do not week by week advance into new high ground.

The opposite state exists at the bottom of a bear market. The public shows not the least interest in Wall Street, and business being usually at its lowest ebb, outsiders do not and cannot see a possible turn three, six or nine months ahead. Big interests scent the possible change, and in any event are prepared to accumulate as soon as tempting values appear. Small stable investors might begin, and often do create a turn at the bottom, by buying for cash small share lots. The "big fellows" might not be in the market at the bottom; they often prefer to play quite freely by confirming future conditions, the money, supply, the banking sentiment, and the feelings of market leaders before they commit themselves definitely. The published trade reports, business conditions, and the aggregate of financial items called "news" is usually of the bluest indigo at the very bottom, and when all are convinced that the country is going to the dogs interest is at its lowest ebb; the market is entirely inactive, those symptoms indicate that the turn has come again.

The student may not care with his limited capital to commit himself then and there; he may not recognize "the turn" so easily. He may miss the chance of buying at the very bottom, but if he begins to think and act in terms of optimism, he will be (to use a vulgarism) "coppering" the majority and doing the opposite, and it is the *minority* that gains the most in Wall Street. Join the minority.

A word more is necessary to give another unfailing sign of the turn at the bottom. Extravagantly low prices are often predicted for certain former leading stocks. We have heard of "Steel going down to 50" when it was around 80 in the 1921 markets; another trader put in a G. T. C. order to buy 100 Crucible Steel at 25, and 100 Mexican Petroleum at 50. He was trying to be "A Specialist in Panics" we presume, but he claimed quite modestly to be an expert in the market, and expected such prices without any thought of panic. The writer believes that our wonderful Federal Reserve System, the banking system in general, and the capacity of the country in general as business leader of the world greatly reduces the probability of a panic. The market had every chance in 1914, 1917 and 1920-1921 to stage a panic—but didn't. We would have the student of this little book not look for extremes in depressed times, but to be satisfied with assured values, low prices, and substantial yields on high grade dividend paying stocks as the limit of opportunity in these times.

The turning points come over and over again in the shorter swings several times a year. They are not radically different in substance and character from the kind experienced at the beginning and end of the minor cycles. They only differ in degree and duration.

Turning Point in Short Groups

Stocks do not go straight down; they seldom or never go straight up. In a bull market it is essential for the pools to maintain a fairly liquid position because they are mostly operating on money borrowed from the banks or financial interests, and banks do not make long-time loans! The banks and financial interests like to see their loans reduced from time to time, and in any event it is expedient for the operators and pools to take profits frequently, to go short on the big bulges, and to reaccumulate on the fairly substantial declines. However, a true bull market will run its course; seldom a reaction wipe out more than a third of the gain in the early stages. During the first six months of a bull market it pays to stay with it entirely; and the turn will come again on the upside when after a sizeable reaction which may last a month or more the averages will go higher than the preceding high point in a true bull market.

Many traders buy during a bull market when a stock gets into "new high ground," with a stop loss order protecting the transaction placed a couple of points below the low price established immediately preceding the rise. The theory is: hold on so long as your stock does not go through this crucial point, the point of resistance. In going short the same rule applies. If a stock seems to have been unable to go through a certain level for many days or weeks, and suddenly breaks, it has met *resistance*, viz., selling pressure at the point of repetition of a certain high figure. After the break it should not have the strength to go through this point again; if it does, all conclusions as to resistance would be wrong. But the unexpected often happens, and a stop loss order, usually from 2 to 3 points above the observed point of resistance, will answer the purpose.

The shorter swings, lasting from a few days to a week or two, are more difficult for the beginner to follow. Frankly, we believe that anyone having less than from five to ten years' market experience should not attempt to trade in and out during such swings. The manipulation is more intense at such times, and the degree of confusion existing for the novice's benefit out of proportion to the possibility of profitable operation. The short turns really create a small cycle within the cycle. The best guide is the volume and activity, and in special movements which occur in individual stocks regardless of the rest of the market, it pays to follow the line of least resistance as revealed by the will of the stock itself to go up or down. It does not pay to buy on a decline merely because a special issue "looks cheap," due to another bad break on top of several others; such a stock is *weak;* not cheap. It is better to allow the movement to culminate, or avoid it altogether. Guesswork and the temptation to buy because a stock *looks cheap* is the cause of considerable loss to even those of fair experience.

A big dividend on a stock that declines to ridiculously low levels is a sign that something is wrong almost invariably. If it is a leading stock, the suspicion is the stronger because the big interests assumed to be back of the company have sufficient money, friends, and backers to support their dividend payer down to reasonable levels. It resolves

itself into this admonition: do not in Wall Street
try to get something for nothing; it might succeed
about once out of every hundred times—certainly
not more often. About a 100 to 1 shot is a poor
chance to take.

CHAPTER VII

How to Detect Liquidation

Typical Condition of a Bear Market—What to Look For

BY liquidation is meant not merely selling and profit-taking in a temporary way. This goes on in the market *all the time*. Transactions running into the hundreds of thousands of shares daily are, quite obviously, not all for buying account. For every share sold there must be a *buyer*, and for every share bought there must be a *seller*. The author has frequently been in a board room among the traders and listened to the conversation (one cannot help hearing!) among the rank and file. In general, those who voice their beliefs aloud are *not* professional traders, though they do nothing else for a few months or a few years but trade. The professional trader, the man who swings more often 1,000 shares at a clip, and is probably long or short of from 10,000 to 15,000 shares at a time, is entitled to be called a professional. Such

men do not talk much. Should they profess to be
bullish, their fellow professional traders will sus-
pect the motive for talking, find out in what stock or
stocks the talker is operating and do him considerable damage. Nothing hurts the operator so much
as unconsidered talk and scattered opinions, because
if he is not believed it does him no good, and if he
is truthful and is believed—well he is a philan-
thropist, or a good samaritan, or a jolly good fellow
—he has no right to be a stock operator.

Coming back to the board room coterie we will
hear, "Ah, there they go—they're selling 'em again.
They're peddling that 'Stude' again—there goes another 100 at three-eighths, a quarter, an eighth!
Sell 'em—sell 'em." Haven't you, dear reader, heard
it? Of course, we can judge the market position of
the commentator very easily; he is short of the market and probably short of Studebaker itself, or he
would have noticed many other things. He might
have noticed, for instance, that this little decline
brings no selling, no "following," in the rest of the
list; that Steel and Baldwin have each advanced one-
quarter and an eighth, respectively; above all, he
would have considered that each transaction over the
tape also represents *a buyer*.

Liquidation is not to be judged by isolated transactions in individual stocks which might arise from special causes. A pool can be in difficulties, his banker in a bad mood some day, or the latter might be prodded by the higher ups in the banking world (banks also have their bankers); a house sponsoring an issue can get into difficulties through being overextended, and finally traders might desire to lighten their load and do a little selling all around, which is often accompanied by short selling.

What is Liquidation?

Profit-taking, then, as well as moderate selling for special reasons and short-selling, is not liquidation. It is very far from that state of general liquidation that causes the big declines that run from a point or two in the market averages to five or seven points within a month or so in the averages. Liquidation means real selling, *and selling at the market*. The first spell is always accompanied by heavier volume than on the average has been recorded in many days. It often follows a dull, listless market where the public is either not taking hold, or is already "loaded up." Any adverse factors, even of a temporary character, suffice to bring about those more serious turns we call liquidation—selling in quantity and volume—by important interests. It is really the quality of the selling and its size that determines the character of liquidation.

Liquidation can take place in a single group like the steels, oils, or motors without immediately affecting other stocks in different groups, but in time they will begin to tell the story. Thus in the summer of 1923 overproduction in California, lower profits for the oil companies, and other adverse trade factors—followed as nearly always—by extravagant speculation of the oil stocks, and consequently inflated prices for most of them, and not least the fact that various recapitalizations in the Standard Oil group and elsewhere resulting in millions of shares outstanding, issued and distributed—not necessarily a direct result of manipulation—resulted in a wide, scattered and weak public following.

Many so-called "pools" are usually formed at such times, and were formed in the oil boom of 1922-1923. They are not uniformly well informed, not uniformly strong, and certainly not consistently or necessarily inside pools. These interests constitute a menace no less than the lightly fortified individual trading on a margin. These people, the evidence is clear, found themselves hung up with some high-priced Cosden, Producers & Refiners, Phillips Petroleum, Marland Oil, and—we judge—

a raft of recapitalized Standard Oil Stocks.

Now the Standard Oils are in the main one of the best and safest groups for permanent investment. The recapitalization may tend to give them a broader and more universal appeal, resulting in record high prices some day, which, in the aggregate, taking into consideration the recapitalizations and old prices, may result in large profits to the investors who can "carry through." But to speculate in them, as many did in 1922-1923 at the mercy of trade changes, and the lenders of money, and the financiers of the pools who saw only the sky as the limit to prices, the first adverse wind, gasoline reductions, diminished demand, selling by old investors who did not wish "to follow the crowd," sufficed to drive the good ship Speculation in Oils on the rocks.

When All Groups Are Affected

Such general liquidation brought on, as it nearly always does, similar *good selling* in groups affected, or identified with the selling pools, either directly or indirectly. The motors followed, and naturally thoughts turn to tires and accessories, which of course go down—as they did on this occasion— with the rest. A lower average market level is thereby established all round. Three or four weakened groups suffice to do this. Other groups join in the decline. The customers—hundreds of thousands of them—holding millions of shares on margin find their accounts depleted by the successive smashes in the groups in which they hold stocks. The average customer, bear in mind, may hold anywhere from three to twenty-five varieties of stocks, and a lower general average for the whole market is *bound* to affect him. If it doesn't he has just been an isolated exception to the rule. Margin calls are sent out throughout the country. Customers respond, the market becomes stabilized, and prices go up. The shorts again get busy. The professional short interest is alive to the margin man's doings; if he does not judge a big margin day by the action of the market itself, it is pretty generally known in Wall Street that "many margin calls went out today." People do not hold their tongues. Brokers are not custodians for each and every one of their employes, and the employe does not know that he is violating a confidence by mentioning quite confidentially to his best friend that "the firm sent out a jag of margin calls today." We need not pause to consider how the big pools judge or actually find out. The business is too big to be locked up as sacred secrets in men's breasts.

After days and perhaps weeks of restored confidence brought around by the spectacle of temporarily higher prices hundreds of thousands find themselves relieved that their accounts are now on safe ground, and they buy a little more as the averages go up. They are in a position perhaps to draw down the margin they put up a month ago—*but they do not; they buy more.* Another week or two and bull conditions again prevail, on the surface. Meantime the original liquidation proceeds on a scale until it is seen that all buyers' requirements are supplied. Dullness may or may not follow, but activity will come again, and in easier stages the previous lows will be approached and broken through. The liquidation again becomes general and goes to a substantially lower level because the outside selling does not come until the fortification of the previous margin call is weakened or removed. It again takes points in the averages as a whole to induce further margin calls. These may be met by buyers, not with enthusiasm perhaps, but still nevertheless with a certain degree of confidence. The newspapers talk of a healthy reaction, or the tail end of the last liquidation, and brokers' letters may feature a "double bottom" or "a shakeout" (if they

are technical), or may encourage their customs in
all honesty.

The Broker

It should be remembered at this stage that the
brokerage element must necessarily prefer to be
bullish and optimistic. They are the distributors of
American and international securities; without them
free markets and the financing of industry would be
quite impossible. Again, we record with pride and
thankfulness that the American investor and speculator is at heart *a bull;* he believes in securities, in
the future of American industry, and does not and
usually will not "let go" of his securities until circumstances place pressure on his brokers, and the
brokers pass the responsibility on to the margin man,
and thence to the investor. Therefore, the largely
bullish emanations from brokerage and financial
sources—the natural course for them to follow.
Since the customer is habitually a buyer, business
can only be done when he buys; it is most volumi-
nous when prices are high; he changes, switches, and
buys again in bull markets, and in declining markets
just waits and hopes—which places no business and
the essential commissions in brokerage treasuries still
struggling against an overhead which is not mobile

nor geared to weeks and months of "nothing coming in and everything going out."

The second margin call may be responded to in part. The second spell, real liquidation, induces outside selling and more speculative short selling. The latter is not vigorously covered next day or on the succeedings days, and at this point in all probability the bigger short interest commences to build up. The shorts grow bolder, and when they are in command they force further liquidation. If the short interest, and pools specially formed to take the short side (if they can borrow stock), succeed in making a final break, which is almost as serious as general liquidation, the third, fourth or last margin call is usually *not met,* and the bulk of the outside speculative following—ninety per cent bulls— are "wiped out."

Liquidation goes no further than this as a general rule. Sellers are there to get good prices. Inside interests, the big pools, institutions and capitalists can usually wait for a better opportunity. They might even at this stage decide to add to their lines. The public does not follow up the resulting rise and "the following" has been exhausted financially, and their confidence is lost. But many bears cover, stronger bearish interests sell *them* some more on the rallies, and if the rally goes to any extent, a moderate amount of liquidation may come in again, which again halts the decline and succeeds in creating another turning point.

It will be seen that at certain stages the public is either waiting hopefully (after complying with margin calls), the original bulls, insiders, remnants of bull pools, and scattered interests are also standing by. Meantime the professional traders in pursuance of the urge to earn a living, failing the commission business which ordinarily comes in, turn speculators mostly from day to day. These people buy or sell in the morning and usually clean house in the afternoon.

No deliveries are called for on Saturdays, so that transactions on Friday are never settled till the following Monday. Yet many of the more conservative professionals prefer to "clean up" over the week end, preferring not to take the chance of serious developments if they are long, or "good news" if they are short being given to the world in the long 46 hours between the closing of the session at noon on Saturday to the opening at 10 a.m. Monday.

CHAPTER VIII

How to Detect Short Selling

THE position of an operator must often, of necessity, be short when he is working on the bull side, because if he is not short he has to use his own money to support the stock, and when he begins that sort of thing there is no telling how soon he will be found "holding the bag"—that is, trying to support the price against whatever offerings of stock might come in. He reserves his real buying power for a bad decline which might put his serious stock way below any reasonable valuation of its shares. Meanwhile his real supporting orders are merely the coverings of the stock he has previously sold short on bulges; hence, covering these shares he is not only taking a profit but is supplying the real foundation for confidence on the part of public and professional traders who, seeing the support, are more tempted to go in and buy again.

While the public is buying on bulges the manipulator is usually taking a short position. This, of course, is one reason why the public is not so suc-

cessful as the experienced operator. The latter does
the reverse of the public, which again illustrates the
fact that the correct way to trade is to observe
closely or, at least, refuse to go with the public—
even to doing the reverse. If the public is buying
on bulges, you should sell; if the public is liquidating heavily in a declining market, that is one of
the best times to buy, for in this business it is the
experienced against the inexperienced traders, and
the latter outnumber the former thousands to one.

When a pool is formed, or large interests accumulate to sell, the price, almost without any exception,
must be put to a level where it will accomplish many
things. It must be made active. There must be a
floating supply to furnish the demand, so that sellers
(even short sellers) must be found or created in
order to "make a market." A stock that merely
goes up and stays up is not attractive to anybody—
not even the investor. It mus thave "swings," even
if these have to be created by selling, and often by
short selling. The original pool or pools in selling
short at certain stages are not necessarily bearish
at that point, but it is part of the engineering. They
make a stock attractive on the declines, and provide
themselves with capital, and a buying power on the

way down—also with the means of combatting those who do not agree by buying against them.

It may seem peculiar that a man who is trying to advance the price of a stock should endeavor to attain a position on the short side almost from the beginning of his operation, but it is true that among the inner circles where stocks are handled and markets are made the technical strength of an issue is sometimes measured by the number of shares the pool is short, even though he is openly and actually working on the bull side. The reason for this is that in an operation for higher prices the support that is given a stock is a most important factor in bringing in outside buying, preventing short selling, holding traders on the long side and gradually increasing the public following.

It is an old truism that markets are *put* up but they *fall* down. This means: When a pool or an operator starts to work in a certain stock, he gives it strong support at rising prices. Each day his supporting level is lifted a little, and it is not until he has been able to dispose of a quantity of stock that he partially withdraws that support and places light scale buying orders on the way down in order to take advantage of any weakness. He is always willing to take back what he has sold, but unless there is some special reason he will not take it back at the same price—only at lower figures.

The Element of Support

In the absence of this support a stock is "hollow underneath"; that is, there are few buyers on the way down. No large operator lets a stock get into this condition unless he is anxious to see it decline in order to enable him to cover shorts or repurchase his long stocks to advantage.

Of course a great deal of the support that is present in a stock may be artificial, and a stock may be held at a certain level by the placing of large buying orders within a fraction or a point of the real supporting level, so that floor traders and specialists may see that there is ample buying power underneath it. This also discourages raiding. Such support is good only so long as it lasts. Upon any sign of general weakness in the market it may be withdrawn.

As an illustration, let us suppose that a certain stock is totally inactive around $30 a share and that an operator takes hold of it. In a few weeks he marks it steadily up to $60. When it reaches the latter price, its earnings and outlook may be no better than when it sold at $30, but the steady and persistent rise in the price of the stock will bring in an increasing amount of buying until, in the upper ranges, transactions may amount to 50,000 shares a day, whereas when it started up they did not total 500 shares a day. Suppose at this stage the operator distributes a lot of the stock and sells it short and then withdraws support and gradually succeeds in dropping it back to 30 again. Those who bought on the way up or near the top will begin selling out. Many will sell the stock short when they see weakness and lack of support, and this short interest will increase and probably reach its greatest proportions when the stock gets back to $30 again (assuming such a theoretical operation). The very people who were talking most bullishly and probably knew the least about it when the stock was at $60, will be found among the loudest of the bears at the bottom of the return trip. This indicates that nothing is more potent in producing buying than a steady upward march of a stock, and nothing induces investors and traders to sell out and go short so much as a steady and persistent decline.

Summed up, the main objective of a distributive bull pool, or a similar individual interest, or a firm having the marketing of a new issue, is to distribute his specialty at rising prices on a scale up, at an

average good price that will show a profit—to himself or his principals, or the selling corporation.
This cannot be attained without marking up substantially, attracting a following, and supporting by
short sales made on the way up, and even attracting
an *outside short interest.*

In a strongly sponsored issue, or a standard leading stock in the initial stages of a bull market, the
early short selling is nearly always by the inside
interest. Its tendency to rebound strongly will indicate that it is well in hand, and should not be
tampered with (on the short side) by the inexperienced. In selling short it should be remembered
there is no theoretical "top" to any stock, because
a short interest can be created where more than the
entire floating supply of the stock is sold short, and
contracts therefor held by inside interests and their
friends. Such a condition is often shown in a declining market when an individual stock shows unexplained strength, rising steadily on *small sales,*
and omitting fractions sometimes in its rise. The short
covering is then said to be urgent, and no reader
should participate in such a stock—either long or
short. If he decides to "go long" on the theory that
the poor or insiders will run in the shorts much
higher, there is a possibility of the shorts settling

privately at any moment; then the stock would have a serious break. Overnight bad developments (news), or pressure brought to bear either by bankers or officers of the corporation to avoid giving their stock a bad name, pressure brought to bear by the Governing Committee of the Exchange on which the stock is listed—any of a dozen factors—a collapse can be caused in spite of an apparently impregnable technical position.

When Stock Is Cornered

"Corners" naturally enter the subject of short selling. The Stock Exchange does not allow its privileges to extend to stocks not having a *free* and *open* market, which means in the large that every listed stock must depend for its price on natural supply and demand. The exchanges will not interfere merely because a stock is ridiculously high, because the buying public may disagree as to value and insist on paying "dear." Bethlehem Steel and General Motors reached what seemed to be ridiculous prices between 400 and 800. They might have been worth it on book values and then current figures (war earnings), and they *could* have gone to twice those figures without calling for corrective exchange action. Most of you have heard of the

Northern Pacific corner brought about by E. H. Harriman, fighting for control of that road in an attempt to squelch the combined Northern Pacific —Great Northern—Burlington ambitions of the Hills, which seemed to be a menace to Union Pacific and Southern Pacific, controlled by Harriman. Northern Pacific ran up steadily from $100 to $1,000 a share and incidentally started a panic. But the settlement price to the trapped shorts was only $250 a share, so anyone who followed up the rise, well knowing that it was engineered, well knowing that millionaire "shorts" were arrayed against it, would have lost out. The General Motors and Bethlehem run-ups in the war market was really a demonstration against the shorts. We have seen the same thing in recent years in Houston Oil, General Asphalt, Keystone Tire, and the "real thing" in the famous Allan A. Ryan corner of Stutz Motor from about $100 to over $700! This is what we mean when we say that there is no real top to a stock, as it might get itself into a temporarily cornered position. Mexican Petroleum often bore the semblance of a cornered stock; it probably *was* rigidly "controlled" between 250 and 300; any stock that rises in a year or so from well under 100 to nearly 300 is in this position. In following a demonstration against the shorts a stop order 5, 10, or even 20 points up will not contradict your judgment but often prevent disaster.

When a closely held stock outstanding to the extent of between 100,000 shares to not more than 500,000 shares rises suspiciously against the tendency of its own group, the inference is nearly always—short selling. This was demonstrated in Crucible Steel, which advanced from the 50s to 278½ between 1918 and 1920 and dropped below 50 in the following year. There was, it is true, a 50 per cent stock dividend, and the latter price was ex, that dividend, which made it the equivalent of 75 against 278½.

A vast amount of short selling comes from the kind of individual or interest known as "the sold out bull." A man or pool may have been bullish on ABC Motors at 50 and stayed bullish till a price of 80 is reached, and then he sells. The stock advances later to 90 or 100, and the seller at 100 "cannot see" this price, does not think the stock is worth it, and his vanity (perhaps also his cupidity) is piqued. He proceeds to go short. Every subsequent reaction confirms his view, so that whether the stock goes back to 80 or climbs to 120 he is short of it. He may be compelled to cover around 120, but he will attempt at some time to get a short position in it. Very often he will be among the most enthusiastic of the bears if the price drops below 80, and he will sell stock all the way down to 60. He may prove to be right; or the original pool may not be interested further, in which even Mr. Short Seller will, in popular language, "get away with it."

We would mention a type of short selling that has been much justified by pools and distributing interests. It is the intention of going short at some stage, preferably near the top, if an issue has been extensively sold and it is desired to give friendly buyers a measure of protection afterwards. Of course, a man has little excuse for taking a tip to buy 100 flexible Rubber at 30, and seeing it advance to 50, where he refuses to take his profits. It goes there, remains dead for a while, and makes a final advance of 10 points to 60, where activity is intense —only confirming the buyer of 100 at 30 in his convictions. The operator who is handling the market on that stock keeps FR extremely active and takes a very substantial short position on it. He knows he need only cease operating and pull out his bids to cause the initial decline that will start the highly inflated rubber ball rolling down the hill again. It might go down at 40, where more buying comes in (including the holder at 30 and his friends), and a drop to 30 and below causes some "explanations" about trade conditions, general market decline and the like. If the operator cares at all about what happens, or his reputation, he will now encourage outside shorts to follow a further decline to 20, and even 15—and in good time, provided with his own funds (profits on the long side plus profits on his shorts), he can do virtually as he likes with his specialty. This kind of a short interest is a useful device, a stabilizer at times, and a club to prevent outsiders tampering with the original operator's market.

CHAPTER IX

How to Detect Pool Operations

Various Conditions Under Which This May Be Done

THE first essential to understanding the movements of securities influenced by deliberate guiding hands is to distinguish first between a natural market, where nothing but supply and demand regulates the daily, weekly or monthly price movements; and second, where forces are at work either to keep the stock alive and active, or give it a stable market (buyers and sellers always on hand), or for the purpose of depressing it for accumulation, or advancing it for distribution.

One of the best assets a security can possibly have is good sponsorship in the market. This is a thing apart from efficient management in a corporate way. By good sponsorship we not only mean strong and able market operators handling its quotations and taking care of the buying and selling demand that comes into most of the active listed stocks at all times. These things are often taken care of during market extremes by active pools; bull pools giving the initial and intermediate rise, while bear pools are formed if the stock is temptingly high and sufficient of it can be borrowed daily to enable these people to safely maintain a short position and be sure of covering at any time they may desire.

What Is a Pool?

A pool in a stock is, after all, not much different to one or more individuals *pooling* their resources, and appointing a single one of their number to conduct the campaign on behalf of all of them. If you and a half dozen wealthy friends get together and put up a few hundred thousand dollars you would be able to form a small bull pool in a few thousand shares of an active stock, provided your manager was able to finance the operation on a 20 or 30 point margin. The average big pool has no greater guaranty of profit and it has the same liability to incur a loss as the individual, or the individual plus his friends forming an unofficial pool with this possible exception:

Example of a Pool Operation

BOUGHT:		SOLD:	
20,000 originally accumu- lated at avg. 45.	$900,000	5,000 at 45¼..$226,250.00	
5,000 at 43	215,000	8,500 at 49⅜.. 419,687.50	
8,500 at 45¼	384.625		
2,500 at 45	112,500		
5,000 at 45	225,000		
41,000	$1,837,125	13,500	$645,937.50

NET LONG POSITION, 27,500 SHARES
AVERAGING PER SHARE, $43.31

The big bull pools consist of influential men able to get more information and knowledge of present and future conditions in business, as well as the corporation whose stock they are buying and selling. Their manager is usually a man who has done nothing else all his life except operate in the market. Naturally he and they are less likely to go wrong; but they do go wrong at times, and suffer big losses. However. to be right six or seven times out of ten operations is to be "ahead of the game," as the expression goes in the Street, and this is all that professional operators and speculative market interests hope to do.

There is another kind of accumulating or purchasing interest not to be confused with pools. The latter exist solely for the purpose of speculative operations in stocks, or to create and keep the market stabilized for future operations. We refer to syndicates formed for the purpose of conducting special financial operations, such as underwriting new enterprises, purchase of a property, holding for resale, the flotation of bonds and stocks and the various undertakings engaged in by banking houses, groups of operators, and financiers generally.

The public is apt to figure that "news" (which isn't *new* to insiders) will influence the price of stocks. This is placing the cart before the horse. the price movements influence the news; they *precede* the news at least nine times out of ten; they anticipate coming news weeks and months ahead; the only kind of news—real news—they cannot and do not anticipate is floods, earthquakes, and acts of God generally. They even anticipate wars! So without devoting many pages to explaining the why and wherefore of this peculiar phase of stock market operations, let us content ourselves for the time being with knowing that the news, or rather the publication of something that has already happened (known in advance to the pool very often) is a collateral accessory before the fact, and the student has only to ask himself: "Is this discounted; is it already anticipated in the present price of the stock;

will the pool try to get a bigger following and put their stock higher, or will sophisticated sellers act on the theory that 'the news is out' and sell?" More often than not a stock declines, sometimes permanently and nearly always temporarily after the publication of an anticipated piece of good news. Conversely, if after a long decline, preceding anticipated passing of dividend for example, once the directors have met, passed the dividend, and the news comes out over the news ticker and the papers, beyond a last selling spasm by belated holders, light speculators, and a few uninformed people, all other factors being favorable, the stock should and does usually go up. It seldom goes into a long secondary decline after this act. We suggest the student note this last piece of information carefully for his future guidance.

A Typical Operation

We have already illustrated a hypothetical operation in Reading stock. Let us examine the workings of a pool in any stock (not necessarily Reading) and get down to the fundamentals, and the mechanics of a pool operation—a fairly typical one.

Suppose, for example, that a large operator believes that a certain stock is selling below the price justified by circumstances, its earnings, dividends, etc., warrant, and more particularly its market outlook. If it be selling at 50 and the operator believes that within a while a price of 75 be justified; if left to itself the stock might gradually climb to that figure, but securities offering good opportunities for profit are not often left to themselves. They need personal direction, and the large operator becomes self-appointed for the task. By explaining the strong points in the situation to his financial friends he is able to induce them to join him in the formation of a pool to operate say in 50,000 shares. The pool is formed by each member putting in whatever amount is necessary to make up say $1,000,000. Various individuals underwrite the amount needed, in sums ranging from say $10,000 per person—sometimes more—sometimes less. In this way numerous individuals are joined together for this particular market operation and the sole discretion is left in the hands of the operator first mentioned—the pool manager.

With the $1,000,000 paid in and the papers all signed giving him the proper authority, he proceeds to carry out his functions as pool manager. As this is a bull pool its operations must necessarily be principally on the long side, but he may believe that by depressing the stock he can accumulate his line nearer 45 than 50. His first operation may be to go short. Frequently those who are invited into pools of this kind buy a little stock on their own account on the side, believing that as this is a bull pool, the stock is sure to go up from the very start. Frequently such individual operators find that they are buying stock for their own account from the manager of their own pool, because he has a little different idea as to the way the operation should start. The individual operators may, therefore, find themselves long at 50 and within ten days the stock may be selling at 45. The pool manager did not guarantee to put it straight up from 50 to 75. He undertook to make a profit; so anyone who makes the mistake of following too closely on what are supposed to be the heels of the pool manager is frequently disappointed.

Assuming that the manager breaks the stock down to 45 by first going short of it, and then offering it down until he induces liquidation from outsiders, he may keep the stock lying between 42 and 45 for several weeks; he may avoid trading it in; he may not bid for a single share; but as stock comes into the market, possibly some of the stock which the pool member bought at 50 among the rest, he gradually absorbs as much of his line as he can secure without advancing the price. It is easier to tire holders out or to discourage them with the long side of a certain stock than it is to shake or scare them out; hence, a "period of rest and quiet" is one in which the pool manager is able to purchase a few hundred shares here and there, until he has not only picked up 15,000 or 20,000 shares, but has created a short interest among those who have observed the action of the stock and are convinced that it is weak and going lower.

Having reduced the market for the stock to "a sold-out condition," where there are no more shares to be picked up without raising the bid, he then quickly bids it up to 45, taking any shares that he finds. He then makes the stock very active at about that price, and the shorts, seeing this activity, are induced to cover. These buyers are then supplied by the pool manager, who thus takes his first profit by selling at a little above 45 a small portion of the stock taken, around 42.

Press Comment a Factor

While he is selling the newspapers begin to talk about increased earnings, important buying by large interests, and this, combined with the activity on the tape, is what may be known as the first part of the advertising campaign.

Having filled the demand at this level, no more work is done until the stock is again offered down to about 43, where the manager takes on any stock that is offered. This enables him to replace all or part of the stock which he sold above 45, and this profit, applied to his total holdings, marks down the cost of all.

The pool manager's next move is to put other brokers into "the crowd" in which his stock is dealt on the floor of the Exchange. To one group of these brokers he gives orders to buy, we will say, 200 or 300 shares every eighth up, which makes a purchasing power averaging 500 shares at each fraction advance. This creates what is apparently a new demand for the stock. Each of these brokers, while operating individually, has an inkling who the others are, and are careful not to duplicate purchasing power at the same fraction. First, one broker buys 200 shares, and then another buys 200, then the first one endeavors to mark it up an eighth by bidding a higher fraction. As the sales are recorded on the tape, they give the impression that the stock is going to be moved higher. The public or traders through the country will begin to buy 100 shares here and there.

Another broker engaged by the pool broker will supply this hundred share demand, not offering any stock, but selling as the bids appear. He will not sell to the brokers who are buying, but will sell to outsiders. The stock in this way is quickly marked up, say 49 or thereabouts, where a supply of 8,500 shares will appear in lots of, say, 1,500 shares at 49, 2,500 at 49⅛, 3,000 at 49¼, and 1,500 at 49⅜.

If the public demand generated by the previous action of the stock and these transactions in round lots at increasing fractions above 49 should prove sufficient to absorb all of this stock, another broker, called the bid-up man, is sent into the crowd. He steps in and bids 49½ for 5,000 shares or any part of it, taking as little as possible. This gives all the floor traders the impression that the stock is in very great demand, and in many cases this bid is reported to the brokerage offices and transmitted through them to clients. If he is successful in obtaining any portion of this 5,000 at 49½, having established the price, the original pool brokers start bidding the stock up from that price in 100 and 200 share lots. It makes a great difference to the manager of the pool whether he attracts buying by the public or *by the traders,* because the floor traders, if they see a movement beginning to halt, will throw over their stock and thus create a duplication of the supply that the pool manager had made an effective on the way up from 49 to 49½, and the pool manager will thus be forced to protect his stock by taking back at a fraction under 49 what the floor traders sell back to him, forcing him to create another rally in a second attempt to distribute.

If on the other hand, the dominating purchasing power above 49 is by the outsiders, they will not be so quick to throw it over, but are more apt to hold it.

From the above it will be seen that the character of the buying at this stage of the manipulation is crucial, for thereupon rests the success or failure of his part of the operation. The heavy supply previously referred to is created not only by the throwing over of stock bought by traders, but in addition they sell short, and the resulting combined supply may more than offset the purchases by the public; hence, a temporary unstable technical position is created in which traders, gaining courage by a slight weakening, continue to offer the stock down until liquidating sales by others are induced, thus producing what is known as a technical reaction.

Under the circumstances no new buying by the

pool manager will occur until the stock has reacted practically to the level at which the bulk of his stock is carried as collateral on bank loans, which is now, say, 45.

As the traders raid the stock to lower levels, they create a supply which is augmented by stop orders, and thus the pool manager, whose buying is the most important, takes whatever is offered between 45 and 46. If the supply is too great, he will buy on a scale down, increasing his takings as the bottom of the down-swing seems to be approaching, and when the selling pressure is about exhausted he will take whatever there is in sight and bid it up quickly. In case it happens to dip as low as 42, he will buy whatever there is up to 45 and bid 45 for it, which will result in long buying by those who are influenced by his strong bids.

Let us say that the stock is now selling at 45½; and he has recovered all of the 8,500 shares distributed at 49 and above, and about 2,500 in addition. The 8,500 repurchased averaged a profit of about four points, which gives him $34,000 profit to reduce the average cost of his long stock. The 2,500 which he has purchased in addition gives him a total long position of 22,500 shares.

He is now ready to take further advantage of

the favorable position, earnings and prospects of the company. He has acquired less than a quarter of his line, and now cautiously adds to his line in a way that will not advance the price much, buying stock as it is offered and taking "a trading position" meanwhile, with the stock holding between 44 and 47. He will sell on bulges and buy back in dips. In this trading area he will probably accumulate another 5,000, which will give him 27,500 shares. This position may be continued over a period of weeks or months, at the end of which time the stock is in a sold-out condition with little for sale on a scale between 49 and 50. The way is now clear for him to start another upward move.

A Graph of Market Movements

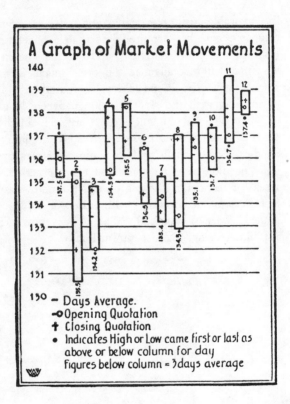

140

139

138

137

136

135

134

133

132

131

130

- Days Average.
- –o Opening Quotation
- + Closing Quotation
- • Indicates High or Low came first or last as above or below column for day
  figures below column = 3 days average